The Ancient Egyptians
A Popular Introduction to Life
in the Pyramid Age

The Ancient Egyptians

A Popular Introduction to Life
in the Pyramid Age

Jill Kamil

The American University in Cairo Press

Dedicated with love
to my daughter Timmy

First published 1976 by
David and Charles (Publishers) Limited, Great Britain, as
The Ancient Egyptians: How They Lived and Worked.

This edition copyright © 1984 by
The American University in Cairo Press
113, Sharia Kasr el Aini
Cairo, Egypt

ISBN 977-424-051-0
Dar el Kutub No. 4047/84
Printed in Egypt by The American University in Cairo Press

Contents

5

Contents

The Three Great Periods

Early Dynastic Period	1st – 2nd dynasties
OLD KINGDOM	*3rd – 6th dynasties*
1st Intermediate Period	7th – 10th dynasties
MIDDLE KINGDOM	*11th – 12th dynasties*
2nd Intermediate Period	13th – 17th dynasties
NEW KINGDOM	*18th – 20th dynasties*
Period of Decline	21st – 25th dynasties
Saitic Period	26th dynasty
Persian Period	27th – 30th dynasties

Introduction

EGYPT's ancient history covers some 3,000 years, from the legendary King Menes (3100 BC), who united the Two Lands of Upper and Lower Egypt, to the conquest of Alexander the Great (332 BC). This period has been roughly divided into thirty dynasties, which have been grouped into three 'Great Periods', as shown opposite.

Each of the three Great Periods bears a distinctive character. The Old Kingdom, the Pyramid Age, is considered by many historians as the high-water mark of achievement. A series of vigorous and able monarchs established a highly organised, centralised government which saw a rising tide of productivity in all fields. It was a culture of great refinement, an aristocratic era, which ended in an explosion of feudal disorder, anarchy and bloodshed. The Middle Kingdom saw the country restored to national discipline by force of arms. The royal house was re-established under strong leadership. Reorganisation throughout the land was immediately reflected in an artistic and architectural revival, massive irrigation projects and a literary breakthrough. This period, when powerful monarchs ruled a feudal state, came to an end when the Hyksos, a warlike people who had settled in the Delta, successfully challenged Egyptian authority. Following the war of liberation Egypt emerged with a strong government and a regular army, heralding an era of international trade and foreign expansion. This was the New Kingdom, when Egypt controlled a vast empire and tributes and booty from the conquered nations and vassal states poured into the state capital at Thebes. It was a

7

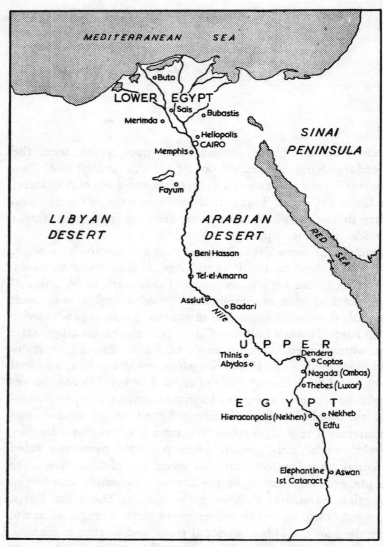

Ancient Egypt

period of unparalleled grandeur, power, wealth and prestige.

The three Great Periods are clearly divided by a period of anarchy when the provincial powers rose against the crown and democratic values were voiced for the first time (1st Intermediate Period) and a period of foreign occupation (2nd Intermediate Period). It is not surprising, therefore, that due to the different political, religious, cultural and social forces at work, each of the cultural peaks should bear a distinctive character. The problem of deciding which should be described as most representative of the ancient Egyptian civilisation is easily resolved. The Old Kingdom is chosen as the classic standard; it was the period in which the hard core of Egyptian thought and institution was formulated; and the time which the ancient Egyptians themselves regarded as a model throughout their history:

After the fall of the old Kingdom, during the 1st Intermediate Period, a sage said to his son: 'Truth (Maat) comes to him well-brewed after the manner of his ancestors . . .' and a priest called Khe-kheperre-Soneb looked back and said: 'Would that I had unknown utterances, sayings that are unfamiliar, even new speech that has not occurred (before), free from repetitions, not the utterance of what has long passed, which the ancestors spake.'

In the Middle Kingdom, when the title 'Repeating of Births' (ie renaissance) was adopted and the monarchs maintained their control over the feudal state by using many of the methods practised in the Old Kingdom, a harper sang: 'I have heard the sayings of Imhotep and Hardedef with whose words we speak so often . . .'

In the New Kingdom the upper classes criticised Amon (the god of the conquering heroes) as the usurper of the 'true religion'. And when Ikhnaton, the world's first monotheist came to the throne he emphasised the connection between his new sun worship and the old sun cult at Heliopolis. In fact he built his sun temples on the same lines as the 5th dynasty temples at Abu Sir. And the symbol of his god, the Aten, was reminiscent of the description of the Sun-god in the 5th dynasty Pyramid Texts: 'The arm of the sun beams'.

9

After the Period of Decline, during the 26th dynasty revival known as the Saite Period, efforts were made to recapture 'the time of the ancestors' . . . . 'for lo, their words abide in writing; open, that thou mayest read and imitate knowledge . . .' And, indeed, the Saite rulers recopied the ancient texts and there is even evidence that they excavated a gallery beneath the Step Pyramid of the 3rd dynasty pharaoh Zoser to see how it was built.

The ancient Egyptians believed that there was once a Golden Age, 'The First Time' when the principles of justice reigned over the land. What was actually meant by this oft-repeated phrase in ancient Egyptian texts is not known. It implies the beginning of an event and was often taken to mean 'The Beginning' or Creation. In fact the Egyptian priest Manetho, who wrote the history of Egypt in Greco-Roman times, saw it as the pre-historic period which was filled with dynasties of gods and demi-gods. 'The First Time' might, however, simply be recapitulations which reflected the Egyptians' pride in their own culture; a confirmation that order once existed. The Golden Age when '*Maat* (Justice) came from heaven and joined those who lived on earth', may be the Old Kingdom civilisation, the purest period of Egypt's ancient history, which rose to its peak and collapsed while Babylonia was still the scene of battles between city states fomented by petty local interests, and while Europe, America and most of western Asia were inhabited by Stone-Age hunters.

LATE AND FINAL
  PALEOLITHIC   12,000–6,000 BC*
NEOLITHIC   6,000–3,400 BC
  Early Pre-dynastic   5,000–4,000 BC
  Middle Pre-dynastic   4,000–3,600 BC
  Late Pre-dynastic   3,400–3,100 BC

FIRST DYNASTY   3,100–2,890 BC
SECOND DYNASTY 2,890–2,686 BC
THIRD DYNASTY   2,686–2,613 BC ⎫ OLD
FOURTH DYNASTY 2,613–2,494 BC ⎬ KING-
FIFTH DYNASTY   2,494–2,345 BC ⎭ DOM
SIXTH DYNASTY   2,345–2,181 BC

First Intermediate Period

* All dates are approximate. The margin of error decreases
as the historic period is approached

11

I

The Country and the People

THE LAND

EGYPT, which produced the world's first great organised society, lies to the north-east of the continent of Africa. It is bounded to the north by the Mediterranean, the south by the First Cataract and to east and west by large tracts of barren desert. The Western or Libyan Desert and the Eastern or Arabian Desert are separated by the River Nile, which emerges from the lakes of equatorial Africa and flows over 4,000 miles to the sea. Ranking with the Amazon and the Congo as one of the three longest rivers in the world, the Nile cascades over Egypt's granite threshold at Elephantine, flows through Upper Egypt, the area lying between Aswan and modern Cairo and then, 200 miles before it reaches the sea, it fans out in a fertile triangle, the Delta, or Lower Egypt. The Nile is the vital artery linking Upper and Lower Egypt. It is also the cause of the great productivity of the Egyptian soil, for it annually brings a copious deposit of rich silt from the monsoon-swept tableland of Ethiopia. Since rainfall in Egypt is almost non-existent and the people are entirely dependent on the river for their crops, it was ultimately on the fertility of the soil that the Egyptian civilisation was based.

In the period known as the Late Paleolithic, large areas of Egypt were covered with forests and savanna. The river, as yet unharnessed, was an alien force. For eons of time it had poured its heavily charged waters over the land. Only the plateau to

12

the west and the mountain range to the east halted its dispersion and accommodated its agitating fury. The distance between them was an average of 7 miles (12 km) and the river left traces of its action in the wearing of rocks and in the colour of its silt on either side. During the protracted climatic fluctuations when the rainfall in Ethiopia lessened, the river flowed with less turbulence and slowly carved its channel. A rich earthy sediment was deposited on each side of the river. The surplus was borne to the north where ceaseless accumulation over tens of thousands of years transformed what was once a bay into a vast triangular morass that formed the Delta.

THE EARLY SETTLERS

Some tribes who tracked game across the grassy plains made their way eastwards. They joined the indigenous people on the plateau overlooking the gorge. Crude flint implements for chopping, scraping, skinning, sawing and stabbing attest to their hunting and fishing activities. Their settlements show that at this time they were little different from Stone-Age settlements in Libya, Morocco and western Europe; populations of African origin that had settled on the Mediterranean. Other tribes made their way westwards from Asia, across the Isthmus of Suez or the Straits of Bab el Mandab.

During the Final Paleolithic the weather became drier. Forests became sparse. The savanna turned to dust. Water holes dried up, and plants withered. The Nile, flowing more sluggishly, deposited ever larger amounts of sediment along its banks. This sediment, and the earth carried to the Delta, was dark in colour and became known as the Black Land, the life-giving land of Egypt, as against the Red Land, the sun-baked desert where life shrivelled and died.

Stone artifacts indicate that at first the different tribal units remained isolated. The changing climatic conditions, however, encouraged them to group together in times of plenty to exploit the valley potential and split into smaller groups during the drought or low-flood season to search for food. As the savanna became a desiccated waste, therefore, the hunting way of life was abandoned, and the people began to adjust to valley conditions; in so doing their lives became unavoidably bound to the rise and ebb of the flood.

The level of the Nile in Egypt began to rise in July each year. At first the water spread over the floodplain lowlands and the people withdrew to the lower valley. Then, as the uplands became progressively submerged they moved to the dry rim of the plateau. The flood reached its full height towards the end of August when activities were limited to the pursuing of hartebeest, wild ass and gazelle on the desert highlands. At the end of October the waters began slowly to recede, leaving behind a fairly uniform deposit of silt as well as lagoons and streams that became natural reservoirs for fish. This was the beginning of the season of abundance. Settlements were made at the edge of the floodplain where movements could be made either into the hills to hunt game animals, or into the floodplain itself which provided ample resources for food-collecting. A variety of plants including wild wheat, brush, bulrush and papyrus formed lush vegetation in the enriched soil, and indigenous and migratory waterfowl were plentiful. In April the Nile was at its lowest level. Vegetation started to diminish. Seasonal pools dried out. Game began to move southwards, or scatter. Fishing was limited to the permanent pools, side channels and the river. But the wooded areas near the river could be exploited for turtles, rodents and Nile clams, which were collected in large amounts. By July the Nile started to rise and the cycle was repeated.

Since the rise and ebb of the flood occurred with tireless regularity, a similar rhythm resulted in the lives of the people who depended on it. This is one of the unique features of the ancient Egyptian civilisation: that the bond between the land and the people, which was established as much by the geographical characteristics of the land as from nature's changeless cycles, affected their essential character. It was a relationship so intimate that it subtly imprinted itself on their lives and beliefs, and ultimately affected their political and social patterns. Though three civilisations rose and fell during Egypt's 3,000 years of ancient history, and these were interspersed with periods of anarchy and bloodshed, foreign occupation, political corruption and centuries of decline, those distinctive features of the culture which were the direct outcome of the natural characteristics of the land endured.

The sun and the river, which together formed the dominating cause of existence, made a profound impression on the people. They were two natural forces with both creative and destructive power. For the life-giving rays of the sun that caused the crop to grow could also cause it to shrivel and die. And the river that invigorated the soil with its life-giving silt could destroy whatever lay in its path or, if it failed to rise sufficiently, bring famine. The sun and the river, moreover, shared in the pattern of death and rebirth: the sun 'died' when it sank on the western horizon only to be 'reborn' in the eastern sky the following morning. And the 'death' of the land followed by the germination or 'rebirth' of the crops each year were directly connected with the river's annual flood. Rebirth was, therefore, a central feature of the Egyptian scene. It was seen as a natural sequence to death and undoubtedly lay at the root of the ancient Egyptian conviction of life after death. Like the sun and the crops, man, they felt assured, would also rise again and live a second life.

The climate in semi-tropical, largely barren Upper Egypt bore no resemblance to the temperate, fertile Delta. And the cultures that developed in each area, like the land itself, each had a distinct character. Agriculture made its first appearance in the Delta, which is not surprising in view of the mild climate and the fact that grain, once planted, benefitted from the natural irrigation of the Nile. In Upper Egypt simple farming communities were also established but due to the more hostile environment the people remained pastoralists rather than farmers.

15

One of the earliest Neolithic sites in Egypt is a large village called Merimda in the western Delta. The houses were oval in plan and made of lumps of clay over a structure of reeds. Grain—a variety of domesticated barley apparently brought from western Asia—was stored in large jars and baskets near the houses. The presence of polished stone axes, fish-hooks and well-made arrowheads indicates however, that the people of Merimda, like their ancestors of the Late Paleolithic, still hunted. They buried their dead around their dwellings. They had few funerary gifts apart from flowers and, in one tomb, a wooden baton. It is possible that this primitive community buried their dead near their houses in the belief that the propitiation of the dead was essential for the welfare of the community—as a form of ancestor worship.

Most of our knowledge of the settlements in Upper Egypt comes from their burial customs, especially from Badari for which the culture called the Badarian has been named. The dead were buried in cemeteries at the edge of the desert. Though no sacred images were found, we know from their simple graves that the people believed in the afterlife, and believed also that this was regarded as a prolongation of life on earth. It may have been the natural desiccation of the bodies of the dead, in the dry heat of the desert sand, into leatherlike figures, that first led the people to believe that preservation of the body was essential for the afterlife. Each corpse was wrapped in matting or skins and placed in a contracted position, knees to chest, surrounded by worldly possessions: bone needles and awls, weapons including spears and arrow-heads, jewellery, including ivory bracelets, necklets, girdle beads and ivory combs ornamented with birds, and fine thin-walled pottery, with black rim or with rippled patterns, containing food, drink and ointments. Buried in the same cemeteries as the people in Upper Egypt, and similarly wrapped, were animals, such as cows, sheep and jackal. The cow later became revered as the goddess Hathor at Dendera. The ram became the god Khnum at Elephantine. And the jackal was later to become Anubis, the god of the necropolis, who was believed to watch over funeral rites and guard the western horizon.

AGRICULTURE AND THE OSIRIS MYTH

In Upper Egypt, therefore, there is evidence of a belief in the afterlife *and* an indication that many of the animals that were to become dynastic gods were, if not yet revered, at least highly regarded. The Delta, on the other hand, yields the earliest evidence of agriculture and indication of ancestor worship, and here the most important legendary figure of ancient Egyptian history, that of Osiris, developed.

The famous Osiris myth is believed in its original form to have been devised to spread an understanding of agriculture throughout the land, explained in terms of the death and re-birth of the corn god. Osiris was probably an early leader in one of the settlements of the Delta who had quite a large following. When he died he became identified with the totem of the area which developed, like many other totems, into a harvest god. Osiris adopted some of the regalia of the older deity including a crown with double plumes and a shepherd's crook, and the agricultural cycle became his domain. He was revered as a god associated with water and the annual death and rebirth of the land.

The Osiris myth underwent many changes with the passage of time. In one form it relates how Osiris ruled the land justly with his wife Isis at his side. He taught his people, as yet partly civilised, the art of making agricultural implements and controlling the waters of the Nile. He also taught them how to take to a corn diet, produce bread, wine and beer. His wife Isis was equally loved and taught the people how to grind corn, weave linen and, with her devotion to her husband, intimated the benefits of domestic life.

Osiris had a brother, Set, who was jealous of his popularity and secretly aspired to his position of favour. Inviting Osiris to a banquet, Set tricked him into entering a coffin specially designed to fit him alone. No sooner had Osiris obliged than Set hastily sealed it with molten lead and cast it on the waters of the Nile where it was borne northwards by the currents to the marshes of the Delta. Isis, grieved by the news of her husband, set off in search of his body. She cut off a lock of her hair and rent her robes in torment as she went on her way following the course of the river. She eventually found the body entangled in the branches of a tamarisk bush. She extracted it and hid it. Unfortunately, Set was boar-hunting and discovered the body, which he brutally hacked into fourteen pieces and scattered throughout the land. The bereft Isis, this time accompanied by her sister Nepthys, once again set out on her search. They found the pieces of Osiris' body, carefully collected them and laid them in a coffin, crooning sorrowful incantations over them to make the body whole.

It is probable that the concept of Osiris falling victim to Set was a comprehensible explanation of the fertile land (with which Osiris was associated) falling victim to the relentless desert (of which Set was the chief deity). The mutilation of the body of Osiris, the corn god, and the scattering of parts up and down the Nile valley, is believed to illustrate the concept of grain sowing, following which, with the necessary incantations, or rural festivals, the stalks of corn would grow again. Be that as it may, the cultivation and storage of grain was a vital factor in the movement away from primitive society towards civilisation. It was a gradual phase of human development. For the assurance of larger quantities of food and food surpluses led to a decline in hunting as an economic activity. Larger groups of people, not all of whom could be crop-growers, were assured of a regular food supply and could settle down. Craft specialisation was a direct outcome, since it absorbed the surplus labour. From the simple technology of the hunters and fishermen we see improved production of weapons, tools and implements and the emergence of new industries including flint mining and flaking.

CULTURAL REGIONALISATION

Gradually the small, isolated, hitherto self-sufficient communities came into contact with one another. They exchanged items produced for items required and a process of assimilation took place. Small groups gravitated towards larger ones or were absorbed by them, and villages coalesced. The sturdy, rectangular brick houses in Upper Egypt were grouped into settlements sometimes covering an area of 120 square yards, surrounded by walls, the grain being placed in large pots within the enclosure. The number of graves in the different cemeteries clearly shows that the people of the Nile valley were fusing into larger social units. These were, in fact, the origin of the various provinces which formed the basis of the political structure of Egypt in historic times.

Late pre-dynastic pottery, like the earlier stone artifacts, indicate that the two cultures of Upper and Lower Egypt continued to exist side by side. The characteristic pottery vessels of Upper Egypt displayed no great change from the Badarian culture from which they developed. They were still largely black-topped and burnished, but new forms had also emerged: some vessels were fashioned like birds and animals; others were decorated with designs of animals, humans and stars; the incised geometric designs were often filled with a white paste, a technique common with other African areas. In Lower Egypt, on the other hand, the characteristic pottery

Black-topped pottery and unconventional pottery with incised geometric designs (Upper Egypt)

19

vessels were either wide-lipped and buff-coloured, with handles in wavy forms that suggest contact with Asia, or decorated with scenes of ritual dances or hunting depicted in red lines painted on the pale pottery.

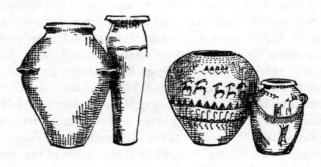

'Wavy-handled' jars and 'decorated' pottery (Lower Egypt)

Some of the Lower Egyptian pottery was decorated with scenes of many-oared ships each bearing a standard surmounted by a totem or emblem. These representations of totem clans are the first evidence of the cultural identity of the various social units. Many of the totems were later established as local deities in the various provinces: two crossed arrows and a shield became symbols of the huntress-goddess Neith of Sais, the emblem like a thunderbolt was the symbol of Min, the fertility god of Coptos near Nagada. There were also standards bearing the emblems of the jackal (Anubis), the scorpion (Selket), the Horus hawk and the Set animal (a dog-like creature with pointed ears and long, upright tail). The latter, Horus and Set, provide the earliest evidence of the mythological rivals, traditionally chief deities of Upper and Lower Egypt.

Cutural regionalisation resulted in the emergence of men who were natural leaders. Their settlements gradually became the central estate, with the accumulations of the others tied to it. That is to say increased trade between the different regions of the Delta led to less and less isolation until the affairs of all gradually became tied to a major estate which represented the richest and most powerful of the settlements. Its leader was regarded as king of the Delta Kingdom and the totem of his area became chief deity. There was a similar tendency towards political unity in Upper Egypt. Whether such leadership evolved without force we do not know. The addition to the weaponry of maces with disc-shaped heads in hard stone, alongside an unusally large number of broken bones among the bodies of the dead, may indicate some intimidation.

THE TWO KINGDOMS

Only towards the end of the pre-dynastic period does an admixture between the Two Lands appear. Lower Egyptian-style pottery was found in Upper Egypt and so was the Horus hawk, traditionally a totem of Delta settlers. 'Followers of Horus' established settlements as far south as Hierakonpolis and Edfu. This does not necessarily presuppose a conquest of Upper Egypt by the Delta. In fact, it seems to have had the direct result of establishing a political awareness of the physical and cultural differences between them, for just before the dynastic period the 'Two Lands' stand out with greater clarity than before. The capital of the Delta Kingdom was Pe (Buto) in the north-west. The leader wore the Red Crown and adopted the bee as the symbol of his kingdom, which included the entire Delta and a stretch of the valley south of the Delta. The Upper Egyptian capital was Nekhen, where the leader wore the conical White Crown and took the sedge as his emblem. His Kingdom extended as far south as the First Cataract. The cobra, wearing the crown of the huntress-goddess Neith, was chief deity of the Delta Kingdom and the vulture-goddess was chief deity of Upper Egypt.

The formation of Two Kingdoms was a vital step towards unification. The early tribes who had settled in the Nile valley, had set traditions and cultural patterns that had at first developed independently of one another. These many social units had gradually coalesced during the neolithic era to form fewer but larger settlements in both the Delta and Upper Egypt. With the federation of the former into a Delta Kingdom and the latter into an Upper Egyptian Kingdom, the country had formed two distinct political entities. It remained to unite them into a single Kingdom of Upper and Lower Egypt.

The unification of the Two Lands was not the result of a single victorious battle, but a slow progress that may have continued for over a century. The aggressive thrust came from Upper Egypt: confined to their long, narrow valley, the Upper

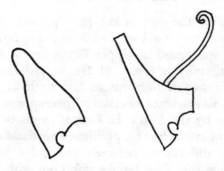

White Crown of Upper Egypt and Red Crown of Lower Egypt

Egyptians sought the fertile expanses of the Delta and moved northwards to more temperate zones. The first leader of whom we have historical evidence is known as the Scorpion King, who left a fascinating record on a ceremonial macehead found at Hierakonpolis (Ashmolean Museum, Oxford). It is carved in three registers. In the upper register is a symbolical representation of the triumph of Upper Egypt over the Delta; dead birds (representing the provinces of the Delta federation) are hung from standards bearing the emblems of the southern tribes. In the central register the Scorpion King, wearing the White Crown of Upper Egypt, breaks ground with a hoe. Behind him are fan-bearers and scenes of rejoicing. In the lower register is a scene of agricultural activities. The events on the macehead are unmistakable records of military triumph. A political victory in the sense of the Upper Egyptians actually adopting the Red Crown of Lower Egypt had yet to be achieved.

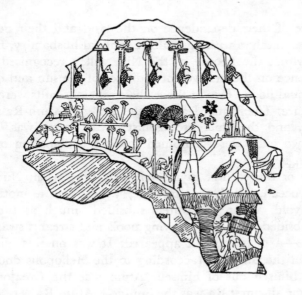

Ceremonial macehead of the 'Scorpion' King wearing the White Crown

SOLAR AND NATURE CULTS

The natural questions of How or Why in pre-dynastic times referred of course only to the immediately surrounding scene. The Libyan desert lay to the west, Sinai to the east. The Cataracts lay to the south and the sea to the north. Above was the sky and below the earth. The ancient Egyptians therefore saw their world as boxed within recognisable boundaries. The sky they believed to be held aloft at the four cardinal points by mountain peaks or pillars that rose above the range forming the edge of the world. The sky was a goddess, the mother-goddess Nut who supported the heavenly bodies and across which the Sun-god travelled each day. The earth was a god, Geb, through which flowed the great river which was believed to rise from the eternal ocean in the south and join the eternal ocean in the north.

Aware of their dependence on the land and their need to sustain themselves with agriculture, animal husbandry, fishing and fowling, the people of the Nile valley recognised their dependence on the benevolent radiance of the sun and on the rich annual flood. Two of the earliest religious cults were solar and nature. The former featured the Sun-god Atum-Ra as the Creator, and the chief protagonist of the latter was Osiris. These two cults were combined into an explanation of The Beginnings.

Some of the earliest myths tell of a time when Nun, the eternal ocean, filled the universe, which was a motionless watery void. When the waters subsided—much as the Nile flood subsided each year, leaving pools and streams swarming with life—a primeval hill appeared. It was on this hill that Atum-Ra the Sun-god (according to the Heliopolis doctrine) created himself out of himself. Atum was the Creator who existed for all time; Ra was the Sun-god. Atum-Ra was, therefore, both the sun and the Creator, who was believed to sail across the heavens each day in a barge, not unlike the papyrus boats that travelled up and down the Nile.

Atum-Ra had four children, all of whom he drew from himself. They were Shu and Tefnut, the gods of air and moisture, and Geb and Nut, the god of the earth and the goddess of the sky. Geb and Nut were at first locked together as one, but on the Sun-god's orders, Shu, the atmosphere, came between them. He lifted the Sky-goddess to the heavens, leaving the Earth-god prone on the ground. Thus was described the watery void, a primeval hill, a Creator and the separation of heaven and earth. When the Sun-god crossed the heavens and cast his rays upon the earth, there was light. And when he entered the underworld at night it was dark and he delegated his power to Thoth, the Moon-god.

Nut the Sky-goddess and Geb the Earth-god had four children. These were the four gods of the nature cult: Osiris, Isis, Set and Nepthys. The Heliopolitan Doctrine or Ennead of Nine Gods therefore comprised:

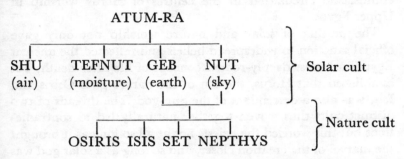

ATUM-RA

SHU TEFNUT GEB NUT   } Solar cult
(air) (moisture) (earth) (sky)

OSIRIS ISIS SET NEPTHYS   } Nature cult

Osiris and Isis had a son, Horus. According to one version of the myth, when Isis and Nepthys prayed over the mutilated Osiris, his breath, hearing, sight and movement were restored and his seed entered Isis and she conceived. She hid herself in the marshes of the Delta until her son Horus was born. He was weakly at first but she cared for him until he was grown and strong enough to avenge his father's death. To rout out Set, his father's slayer, Horus travelled far and wide and many and terrible were the battles between them told in countless myths; in one noteworthy clash Horus lost an eye which he later recovered and presented to his risen father, Osiris, as a symbol of his sacrifice. Horus finally triumphed over Set, took over the throne of his father and was regarded as the ancestor of the pharaohs.

It will be noted that Horus and Set, who first appeared as ensigns on standards, are the protagonists in the mythological drama. They represent good and evil. Set, the desert totem, is cast in the role of the evil brother, and Horus, traditionally a totem of the clans of the fertile Delta, is cast in the role of the devoted son. The choice of 'Horus' for the offspring of Osiris

25

and Isis is most significant. The hawk ensign, as we have seen, was carried to Upper Egypt by 'Followers of Horus' and had probably come to symbolise leadership. If, therefore, the Osiris myth was indeed devised to explain the benefits of agriculture, the tale of the victorious Horus triumphing over the wicked-brother/desert-deity Set, would be assured of enthusiastic circulation in the centres of Horus worship in Upper Egypt.

The uniting of solar and nature worship not only gave official sanction to widespread beliefs and reflected the ancient Egyptians' most deeply-rooted concept of life after death, but established that Horus, the son of the nature gods Osiris and Isis, was also a descendant of the Sun-god. The threads of two distinct cults thus woven together naturally led to contradictions but this worried the priests not at all so long as it brought the marvel of the creation closer, and so long as a solar god was victorious.

The sun cult is apparent, in one form or another, throughout ancient Egyptian history. Its inception as a doctrine, however, cannot be accurately dated. There is no evidence of its introduction in the first three dynasties, yet the political power of Heliopolis which became apparent in the 4th and 5th dynasties (Chapter 3) could never have been so easily imposed or readily accepted had the cult not enjoyed a long and hallowed observance already. We can, fortunately, resort to relative dating, and here we are on firm ground. The Heliopolis Doctrine was established before the Memphite Doctrine, which only developed after the rise of Memphis.

2

How Their World Began and Grew

NARMER, THE FIRST PHARAOH

MENES (the Horus Narmer) is the legendary first pharaoh of the 1st dynasty. According to tradition he managed to gather together the resources of his Upper Egyptian Kingdom and successfully invade the Delta. In subjugating the provinces of Lower Egypt he brought the whole of the Nile Valley under his domination from the First Cataract to the sea. Narmer set up a fortification south of the apex of the Delta near the borderline between the Two Lands. It was known as the 'White Wall', probably in reference to the Upper Egyptian Kingdom it represented, though later known as Memphis.

The legends which have come down to us of Egypt's first pharaoh have undergone thousands of years of embellishment. Traditionally recognised as the founder of Memphis and the Temple to Ptah, its chief deity, Narmer was said also to have surrounded his chosen headquarters with dykes and diverted the river Nile—which hitherto flowed through the sandhills of the Libyan range—through an artificial channel dug between two mountain ranges. It was said, furthermore, that he constructed a lake around the White Wall which was fed by the river. A famous slate known as the Palette of Narmer (Cairo Museum) records his military triumph. Narmer is sculpted in low relief on both faces: on one side he wears the White Crown of Upper Egypt and on the other the Red Crown of

Lower Egypt, thus portraying him as monarch of both king-doms. The reliefs, executed with flair and confidence, show the victorious monarch striking a kneeling enemy with a raised club, inspecting the bodies of decapitated enemies and, accompanied by fan-bearers, symbolically represented as the

Palette of Narmer showing the pharaoh wearing the White Crown on one side and the Red Crown on the other

'Strong Bull' breaking fortifications of a township as he tramples the enemy. The Horus hawk is symbolically depicted trium-phant over the land of the papyrus: the Delta.

EARLY DOCUMENTS

The Palette of Narmer is entirely symbolic in its message. Writing had not yet developed. But there are indications that before the first dynasty isolated miniature images of men, ships and animals depicted on pottery had become pictorial repre-sentations of the objects themselves. Gradually these picto-graphs came to represent phonetic sounds (phonograms) which could be grouped together to form words. In English for example, a bee and a leaf might be combined to read belief; the phonograms had no relation to the original pictorial representation, apart from representing a similar sound. Series of phonograms would form sentences.

Some of the earliest written documents show that the years

Hieroglyphs of 'bee', 'leaf' and 'belief'

were numbered by some outstanding event, often a journey, the erection of a building or some royal ritual. Gradually lists of year-names were kept. These formed the basis of the historic archives, of which the Palermo Stone was the first. Among the five small fragments discovered is a record of the founding of a temple to Neith in Sais in the Delta by Narmer's successor. Neith was a huntress-goddess of the early tribes of the north who undoubtedly had quite a large following by the early dynastic period. In raising a temple to a popular Delta goddess the Upper Egyptian conquerors set a precedent that was followed throughout dynastic history: that of calculated tolerance for political gain. There appears to have been an effort to create a common culture by uniting opposing factions and combining the traditions of Upper and Lower Egypt. Unfortunately the efforts were to no avail. There is evidence of national discord for some 200 years after the so-called unification.

CONSOLIDATION OF UNITY

Resistance against Upper Egyptian domination was undoubtedly aggravated by a natural antipathy between the settlers of Upper and Lower Egypt arising out of their cultural differences. In fact earlier traditions had repeatedly to be recognised in order to emphasise a single rule over the Two Lands. For example the pharaohs (who traditionally bore a 'Horus name') adopted, during successive reigns, a *nebty* or 'Two Ladies' title (which was a combination of the cobra-goddess of Buto in Lower Egypt and the vulture-goddess of Nekheb in Upper Egypt), the Double Crown (a combination of the White and Red Crowns) and a *ni-sw-bity* title which also combined two traditions, being a combination of the pre-dynastic symbols of Upper and Lower Egypt, the sedge and the bee.

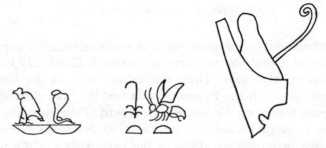

Nebty title, *ni-sw-bity* title and Double Crown combine the traditions of Upper and Lower Egypt

People unfamiliar with ancient Egyptian history find it difficult to realise how vitally important titles are in tracing the course of events. Most of the records and inscriptions of the early dynastic period have perished and little is known of the activities of the pharaohs of the first two dynasties. Yet during this vitally important formative period many traditions were established. For example the Horus name, the *nebty* and *ni-sw-bity* titles, were never abandoned in later periods, though others were added to the royal titulary to denote different loyalties or political currents.

The geographical and climatic differences in Upper and Lower Egypt which had resulted in the development of two different cultures were reflected also in the entire political structure of the country; for despite the effort to weld them together, the 'Two Lands of Upper and Lower Egypt' were to remain two united political entities rather than a single political unit. Dualism was finally seen as unavoidable and was used to emphasise unity. There never was a King of Egypt, nor cabinet, nor treasury. There was a King of Upper and Lower Egypt, a Double Cabinet, a Double Granary and a Double Treasury. Even the 'Great House', the palace, which was the seat of the government, had a double entrance representing the two ancient kingdoms, and the hieroglyph for 'Great House' was frequently followed by the determinative signs of two houses.

It is not surprising, therefore, that the pharaohs of the first dynasty all had two tombs, one constructed on the plateau above Memphis and the other near Abydos in Upper Egypt. These may have represented the pharaoh's dual capacity as King of Upper and Lower Egypt; alternatively the structure in Memphis may have been the actual tomb and that in Upper Egypt a cenotaph where relatives could more easily provide the food offerings for the afterlife. Tomb construction advanced during the 1st dynasty. Excavations indicate that the royal tombs were large, shallow trenches, hewn of bed-rock and divided into a series of chambers by cross walls. The central chamber was the tomb. Others were store-rooms for the provisions for the afterlife: funerary furniture, ornaments, jewellery and games. Some of the underground chambers were brick-lined; others were lined with woven reed mats. The substructure was roofed with wooden beams and planks and surmounted by an impressive superstructure with recessed panelling. The royal tombs at Memphis had large rectangular plaques depicting the deceased at a table of offerings, which became the pattern for representations in funerary temples. The royal tombs in Upper Egypt had funerary stele or tombstones—rectangular slabs, tall and sometimes rounded at the top, placed vertically in the ground and inscribed with the names and titles of the pharaoh.

31

The bodies of the dead were not mummified, in the early dynastic period, but were wrapped lightly in strips of linen. Sometimes the limbs were bound separately and then a bandage was wrapped round the whole body before it was placed in a wooden sarcophagus. Close to the royal tombs were subsidiary tombs, probably of dependants in the household of the pharaoh or artisans in the boat-building, carving, painting and pottery trades. The occupants were possibly interred to serve the king in his afterlife, and may have been killed when he died, whether they succumbed willingly to their fate we do not know, though the lower classes may have believed that to be buried with their masters would ensure them a better after-life themselves.

A 5th-dynasty inscription records the levels of the Nile for every year back to the reign of Djer, the third pharaoh. Since the cycle of agriculture depended on the Nile flood, the time of the inundation was vitally important and progress in astrology was undoubtedly stimulated by the desire to forecast its arrival. It was observed that the rising waters coincided with certain aspects of the stars: when Sothis the dog-star rose with the sun between 19 and 20 July. An ivory tablet dating to the 1st dynasty explicitly mentions 'Sothis, Opening of the Year, the Flood' and a primitive sighting instrument made on a date-

---

Khafre's famous cult statue, carved from diorite

Hesi-Ra, a contemporary of Zoser. The wooden panels found in his tomb show 3rd-dynasty boldness in conception and execution of relief sculpture

Khafre's Pyramid at Giza (taken from the top of the Great Pyramid of Khufu) had limestone slabs in the upper courses and partially unpolished granite slabs in the lower

palm has been found. Once the arrival of the flood could be predicted, its waters could be controlled and channelled. Records of the levels were strictly maintained, at first on stairways built into a wall or quay. Untold years of recording and observation resulted in a 365-day calendar (12 months of 30 days and 5 extra feast days) the basis of which, in only slightly altered form, has descended to us today.

Though little is known of the activities of the pharaohs of the 2nd dynasty it seems that there was even more active resistance against unity. One pharaoh (Per Ibsen) may have formed a breakaway government in Upper Egypt, for he significantly abandoned his traditional 'Horus' title and adopted a 'Set' title: in other words he exceptionally surmounted his royal emblem with the ancient desert god of Upper Egypt. This move of revolutionary proportions was quashed by his successor, who managed to re-establish the Horus tradition in Upper Egypt, and a Horus and Set title was temporarily adopted. Like the *nebty* and *ni-sw-bity* titles, and also the Double Crown, this combined two ancient traditions: Horus and Set as gods of Upper and Lower Egypt.

Triads of the pharaoh Menkaure between the goddess Hathor and different provincial deities bearing the features of the queen, and identified by the heraldic emblem of their districts

REVISION OF THE MYTHOLOGICAL TRADITION

The fabric of ancient Egyptian mythological tradition, which survived in embellished or mutilated form for thousands of years, was woven and rewoven, time and again, to justify new conditions, or explain political trends; it was sometimes even entangled to promote a cause. As the country underwent changes in social and political structure there were accompany-

Traditional Horus 'Serekh' of Sekhemib, Set 'Serekh' of Per Ibsen and Horus and Set 'Serekh' of Kha-sekhemwy, indicating reunification. (See p 35)

ing changes in the myths which, though radical, did not render earlier traditions obsolete. The battles between Horus and Set, the tribal ensigns, for example, not only reflected opposites—fertile Delta against barren Upper Egypt, and good and evil in the context of the nature cult—but equally portrayed the political friction in the early dynastic period, also expressed in mythological terms as battles between Horus and Set. This is why there are so many contradictions and so-called 'discrepancies' in Egyptian mythology, which have unfortunately earned Egypt the reputation of having a 'myth-making' mentality.

The importance of a local deity naturally increased in relation to the size and population of a settlement. When Memphis became the royal burial ground and factories sprang up for the manufacture of funerary equipment, Ptah, a minor local deity, evolved into a patron deity of the arts. The High Priest, who was also the chief artist, promoted his deity as the inspiration behind the metal-worker, carpenter, jeweller and sculptor. However, in the areas surrounding Memphis, two other deities were revered: Sekhmet the lion-goddess and Nefertum a lotus-god. As Memphis expanded it drew these into its orbit. The problem of having three deities in a single area was easily resolved by explaining Ptah as the chief deity, Sekhmet as his consort and Nefertum as his son. United they formed the Memphite Triad. Ptah also absorbed Sokar (an ancient god of the Sakkara necropolis from which the latter name is derived) and became known as Ptah-Sokar.

RISE OF MEMPHIS

Temples were the centres of each community. The priests who maintained them accepted gifts and offerings on behalf of the deities and donations of cattle, fruit from the first harvest and revenue from the land. Deities with widespread appeal naturally amassed most wealth, and the priesthood of Ptah acquired a taste for power. They realised that though Ptah was the chief deity of the Memphite Triad, he had mere local appeal; unlike the Sun-god, whose centre of worship was Heliopolis, Ptah was unknown outside Memphis. If he could acquire solar power, then like the Sun-god he would enjoy pre-eminence. If Memphis could become a centre for culture and learning, then the priests themselves would have power and prestige second to none.

In populous Memphis the priests staged a drama which reveals their ingenious plot to undermine the sun cult and Heliopolis for the greater glory of Ptah and Memphis. The drama was in mythological language, and has miraculously been preserved in a late copy on what is known as the Shabaka Stone. Dressed as deities, the priests acted familiar tales of the creation of the physical world from the waters of chaos; of

37

death and resurrection and of the triumph and coronation of a Horus king; each item of the traditional doctrine was presented, but subtly varied in the interests of Memphis. For Ptah, the priests claimed, was himself the eternal ocean Nun that existed for all time and out of which both the primeval hill and Atum-Ra were created. Therefore their deity Ptah existed before Atum. They explained that the primeval hill rose from the eternal ocean, not in Heliopolis as in the earlier cosmogony, but in Memphis; that Memphis was the 'Great Throne', the site where Isis beheld the body of her beloved husband drowning in the water, and, moreover, the burial-place of Osiris.

The priests did not deny the older doctrine. They merely claimed that since Ptah was the eternal ocean, all other gods were no more than manifestations of him. One can well imagine the impact on the illiterate masses of the sight of the priests dressed up as their favourite deities, Horus and Set, Thoth the Moon-god and Geb the Earth-god, appearing as men and talking together. It must have been a highly inspired priesthood who at one stroke captured the minds of the masses by satisfying their taste for a tale, and swayed the intellectuals through profound abstract reasoning. For they pointed out that Ptah's primacy lay in his power over the heart, or *Ib* (which was the seat of thought and judgement) and the tongue, which represented command. In place of muscular effort (as when Shu, the atmosphere, separated Nut and Geb), they described the heart and tongue as the organs of creation. They explained that all things that originated in the heart took shape on being pronounced. The words on the Shabaka Stone: 'For every word of the god came about through what the heart devised and the tongue commanded,' bear a striking resemblance to St John's opening passage: 'In the beginning was the Word'.

The Memphite Drama, staged in the populous capital, is therefore a fascinating intermingling of mythology on the one hand and abstract reasoning on the other. By giving Ptah credit for the creation of the physical world, for '[giving] birth to the gods, [making] the towns, [establishing] the provinces, [setting] the gods "of every wood, every stone, every clay" in their shrines', the priests of Memphis established themselves as the supreme political power of the state and the custodians of the country's wealth.

Near the borderline between the Two Lands we now have evidence of political rivals: Heliopolis, situated on the eastern bank of the Nile about 7 miles west of modern Cairo, and Memphis on the western bank some 16 miles further south. Each city had a powerful priesthood which claimed for its deity the creation of the physical world. Their two cosmogonies, the Heliopolitan Ennead and the Memphite Doctrine, had as we have seen many concepts in common. Yet the priests of Memphis had not only reinterpreted the earlier and more widely held view of the creation for the greater glory of Ptah, but had also deliberately undermined the centre of the sun cult. Up to this point in Egypt's ancient history the major obstacle to unity between the Two Lands had been internal dissent based on cultural differences. We now have a different problem to consider: which deity, Atum-Ra or Ptah, was the creator of the physical world? Which of the two priesthoods should be looked upon as the guardian of the country's economy?

ZOSER, FIRST GOD-KING, AND IMHOTEP

Throughout the early dynastic period, as we have seen, concord was short-lived. Periods when the 'Two lands were united' and the 'Two gods were at peace' implied recovery from anarchy rather than peace. Although the pharaoh called himself 'King of Upper and Lower Egypt', combined ancient traditions in his titles, and celebrated the 'Feast of the Union of the Two Lands'; although, moreover, the last pharaoh of the 2nd dynasty probably married a northern princess in order to consolidate the union, this unity seemed no more likely to last than earlier efforts. A strong element was needed to maintain it. This was finally achieved by the creation of the dogma of divine kingship which, as will be made clear, simultaneously resolved both the problem of unity and the question of political priority.

The ancient Egyptians had learned to predict nature's patterns and control the crops, nature's gifts. The earliest record of pharonic achievement shows the 'Scorpion King' digging a canal before his rejoicing subjects, and Narmer, the first pharaoh, reputedly diverted the waters of the river Nile. The superimposition of man-worship on nature worship was, therefore, not unfitting. A divine monarch who was neither an Upper Egyptian nor a Lower Egyptian but who ruled as a God-king might finally consolidate the country. Certainly, as a god he would be above challenge and his power would be absolute.

The pharaoh Zoser, whose name is indelibly linked with that of Imhotep, his adviser, administrator and the gifted architect who built his funerary complex at Sakkara, is believed to have been the first God-king. His accession to the throne marks the beginning of the first of Egypt's three 'great periods', the Old Kingdom.

Zoser's name passed into near-oblivion when his body was laid to rest. Imhotep, was never forgotten: scribes of later times made him their patron, his wisdoms were recited for thousands of years, and the Greeks, 2,000 years after his death, identified him with their own god of medicine, Asklepios, deified him and raised a temple at Sakkara where they assumed his tomb to be. Imhotep's architectural genius lies in his use of durable fine-quality limestone to imitate the brick, wood and reed structures which have all perished. It is thus through this surviving monument, the Funerary Complex of Zoser, of which the Step Pyramid is the main feature, that the 3rd dynasty springs to life. Through it we can visualise the contemporary houses, for it provides evidence of how logs were laid across the roofs of houses, how bundles of reeds were tied together with the heads fanning out and probably coated with mud. Imhotep transcribed matting, papyrus and palm-stalk fences into heavy masonry. More important, in his recreation in stone of the actual palace of Zoser in the belief that he could repeat in the afterlife his experiences on earth, we have evidence of the religious practices of the times and—since religion and politics were inseparable—can theoretically reconstruct the political organisation of the country.

The Step Pyramid of Sakkara is Zoser's tomb. It is part of a huge complex comprising entrance colonnade, a Great Court, a Heb-Sed Court, Southern and Northern buildings, a Mortuary Temple and a Serdab, surrounded by a 30ft wall of white limestone. It covers an area of 15 hectares, in a 595yd × 303yd rectangle. Zoser's tomb rises in six tiers to the north. It is

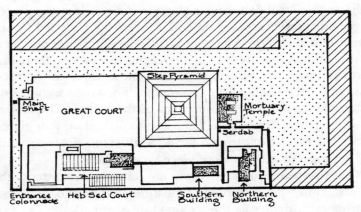

Ground plan of the Step Pyramid complex

approached through the Great Court which contains two B-shaped constructions where the pharaoh ran his traditional Heb-Sed race.

The Heb-Sed is widely believed to be a 30-year jubilee but, in the Old Kingdom, pharaohs with reigns of less than 30 years celebrated it. Its origins have been lost but must date to a time when a leader was ceremoniously put to death as soon as he showed signs that his powers were fading, before the spirit was contaminated by the ailing body and in order that it might pass quickly into the body of a vigorous successor. In a country where hunting had become a sport and where invasions were yet unknown, the pharaoh, whose prestige as a leader naturally depended on aptitude, had to show his prowess in other ways. The race was the running of a fixed course in the presence of his subjects to indicate he was sufficiently competent to rule the nation. Those who witnessed the event naturally recognised the pharaoh's strength and accepted his superiority. The earliest Heb-Sed race was portrayed on seals from Sakkara dating to the 1st dynasty. By the 3rd it had been elaborated from the running of a fixed course to a five-day celebration attended by people from distant parts of the country. Surviving reliefs indicate that local deities were borne in their shrines and placed in the sanctuaries situated on both sides of the Heb-Sed Court. Their number nearly corresponds with the number of provinces in the land at the time. It is interesting to observe, therefore, that the main feature of the celebration, apart from the race, was the re-enactment of the coronation. The king was borne on a carrying-chair by representatives of the gods of Upper and Lower Egypt and performed the coronation ritual four times; each time he was enthroned facing a different direction while the appropriate crowns were placed on his head.

There appears to have been an incentive to attend the festival. Gifts were presented to the different priesthoods. Those bearing such deities as the wolf-god of Assiut, Bastet the cat-goddess of Bubastis and Anubis the jackal-god may have received cattle. The priests bearing Sobek the crocodile-god of the Fayoum, Khnum the ram-god of Elephantine, Min of Coptos, Neith of Sais and Hathor of Dendera may have received personal gifts. Undoubtedly the priesthoods of the two ancient goddesses of Upper and Lower Egypt, the vulture-goddess of Nekhen and the serpent-goddess of Buto (whose symbols formed the pharaoh's *nebty* title), participated in the ceremonies in the Northern and Southern buildings, which are believed to represent the pharaoh's control over the Two Lands.

The ancient Egyptians believed that man comprised different immortal elements including the *Ka* and the *Ba*. The *Ka*, or spirit, was born with the individual, remained united with him throughout his life and continued to exist when the earthly body ceased to function. It was believed to dwell eternally in the vicinity of the tomb. The *Ba*, only coming into existence when the earthly body perished, was the soul and was, at first, probably a concomitant of Divine Kingship. Zoser, as both god and man, had both elements catered for in his funerary complex: the mortuary temple for the *Ba* and the Serdab for the *Ka*. The latter was a tiny stone chamber (the first of its kind) built entirely separate from the tomb and entirely enclosed apart from two tiny holes known as the 'eyes of the Ka House'. Through these the *Ka* of the deceased pharaoh, inhabiting the portrait statue placed therein, could 'see the offerings and smell the burning incense'. The priests in the mortuary temple helped effect the transformation of the soul or *Ba* when, presiding over the body of the deceased, they would chant: 'Rise thee up, for this thy bread which cannot dry and this thy beer which cannot become stale, by which thou shalt become a Ba'.

The emphasis on the 'Two Lands' and their unification is apparent in Zoser's funerary complex: shrines for Upper and Lower Egypt situated on each side of the Heb-Sed Court, Southern and Northern buildings and, in addition, the existence of both a tomb chamber and a cenotaph within the complex (whereas earlier pharaohs had had one at Memphis and the other in Upper Egypt). Furthermore the participation in the Heb-Sed Festival of the various deities of Upper and Lower Egypt, and the spirit of toleration shown them, not only steered the different priesthoods from complaint and discontent, but forced them to recognise the pharaoh as the god *par excellence*.

USE OF LOCAL CULTS TO ESTABLISH UNITY

The development of local cults was undoubtedly part of the political development of the country. The term 'local deity' is, however, confusing. For though some of the ensigns on standards that had distinguished the tribal units of the early settlers of the Nile valley came to represent heraldic images which gave names to the different localities, these were not fetishes, objects of blind devotion. Although the cow might be seen as the seat, or visible manifestation, of a godly force, it was slaughtered for meat. And the lion, though regarded as sacred in certain areas, was unhesitatingly killed in defence. These totems and sacred animals were at first a clan affair.

When Egypt became a single, unified nation, it followed that the totem clans would have to be brought into a mutual relationship with the governing power. A Ptolemaic inscription on a rock-face near the First Cataract records an oral tradition that survived from the 3rd dynasty and reveals, indirectly, how this may have been achieved. It tells of a terrible famine that struck the land in the reign of Zoser. The people were told that they suffered because the gods were angry with them for not providing adequate offerings. The pharaoh Zoser himself made special arrangements for regular supplies to be presented to the people to enable them to curb the anger of the gods. It was only when a totem or sacred animal was declared to be capable of anger and the people felt obliged to placate them with sacrifices that they developed into local 'deities'. Once they inspired fear and awe they became the focus of acts of worship, hymns and prayers; sacred monuments were erected for them and local settlers, who later formed the local priesthoods, were recruited to maintain them. Plants and objects of the area then became the attributes of the newly evolved deity.

It seems, therefore, that in order to bind together the settlers in far-flung areas, the governing power encouraged the develop-

44

ment and practice of local cults by low-ranking local priests, but limited their function and bound together their energies under a God-king whose Heb-Sed festival they attended, and whose divine nature they recognised. It was a policy of promotion and appeasement which served a dual purpose: it enabled a generous and tolerant pharaoh, who provided offerings for local deities to take credit for favourable conditions and, at the same time, it provided scapegoats for disaster—the local gods were angry.

The evolution of cults notwithstanding, the people in the rural areas in Upper and Lower Egypt were not much affected by the politico-religious struggle near the border between the Two Lands. Their lives were controlled, like migratory birds, by the rhythm of the seasons. The flood arrived each year to nourish the soil and yield an ample return from the land, and the sun shone in a cloudless sky. They may, therefore, have assumed that the cosmic and nature gods, whose power directly concerned them, tended to be kind and dependable and their goodwill could somehow be guaranteed. They rose at dawn to work on the land and set aside their tools at sunset. Since the physical features of the land made communication difficult, ideas of the Sun-god and the daily solar cycle varied considerably from one area to another. In one settlement the sun was seen as the right eye of the divine face of Horus the Sky-god, who created day when he raised his lids at dawn, and night when he closed them in the evening. In another, he was the son of the Sky-goddess Nut and the Earth-god Geb who was born anew each day. The sun was variably seen as a hawk in the heavens with outstretched wings taking a daily flight across the sky, or a disc borne on the back of an enormous beetle, Kheper.

No combination or amalgamation of gods should be considered accidental. The various group combinations of Atum-Ra, Atum-Ra-Kheper, Ra-Harakhte ('Horus of the Horizon'), which were used in various combinations to mean 'the Sun-god' were probably the result of a calculated effort

45

to indicate to the people of distant areas that the sun that shone over their settlement was, in fact, no different from the sun that shone in the cult centre of Heliopolis. It was explained that the Sun-god was born an infant in the eastern sky (as Kheper), developed to the peak of maturity at midday (as Ra) and then slowly would lose power until, old and tired (as Atum), he would approach the western horizon. There already existed a strong bond of belief and ritual throughout the land. At dawn each day a prayer was offered in every shrine, whether it belonged to sacred cow, ram, hawk, ibis, vulture, serpent or crocodile, bull, jackal or lioness. The oldest prayer to have survived is a prayer to the Sun-god in the Pyramid Texts:

> *May you wake in peace, O purified, in peace,*
> *May you wake in peace, O Horus of the East, in peace,*
> *May you wake in peace, O soul of the East, in peace,*
> *May you sleep in the Night-bark,*
> *May you wake in the Day-bark,*
> For you are He who oversees the gods,
> There is no god who oversees you.   (*U. 573*)

The effort to unify sun worship by creating a composite deity, alongside evidence of the development of local cults, evinces a movement towards both unity and plurality in the Old Kingdom: one God (the 'Great One') and many gods ('all the gods'). This should not be regarded as contradictory. To establish a unified politico-religious system the ruling power encouraged local religious identity and, by promoting a God-king whose commands had divine authority, limited the jurisdiction of the local priests and justified their own dominance. Unity was the purpose, plurality the method.

3

How They Organised Their World

GOVERNMENT IN THE GREAT PYRAMID AGE

THE centralised government that created one of the high-lights of ancient Egyptian history, the great Pyramid Age, appears to have been established by a powerful ruling élite who promoted a God-king to unite the country as well as sway the politico-religious current away from Memphis. It may well have been the crucial fact of the priests of Ptah having endeavoured to undermine the sun cult to their own advantage that transformed the Heliopolis priests' eagerness to enlighten into an impulsion to control.

Zoser, whose reign heralded an era of boundless vision and invention was a God-king of solar faith. In death he would join, as by right, his father the Sun-god in heaven. His chief official, Imhotep, whose titles included 'First after the King in Upper Egypt, Minister of the King in Lower Egypt and Administrator of the Great Palace' was also 'High Priest of Heliopolis'. Moreover, some fragments of what are known as 'Zoser reliefs' (Turin Museum) which concern the Heb-Sed Festival, refer to the Heliopolitan Ennead (not the Memphite Doctrine). With little to distinguish between religion and politics the balance of power had tilted in favour of the priests of Heliopolis. They controlled trade routes, exploited the mines and handled the country's valuable raw materials including stone, metal, precious stones and copper. Unity having been finally estab-

47

lished, political stability in the 4th dynasty is reflected in economic prosperity, technical achievement, productivity and inventiveness.

The broad administrative pattern of the country was laid in the reign of Senefru. After a turbulent transition between the 3rd and 4th dynasties he secured the throne by his marriage to Hetep-Heres, the daughter of Huni, builder of the first true pyramid at Meidum. Her title, Daughter of God, shows her to have belonged to a family with strong religious affiliations. Senefru, a vigorous and powerful monarch, administered the country directly through members of the royal family. He achieved this by creating the post of Vizier or Prime Minister which became the inherited right of his oldest son by his 'Great Royal Wife'. She carried the direct line of royal blood, her son being legitimate heir to the throne. It is not without significance, therefore, that the first Vizier, Prince Kanufer, was also High Priest of Heliopolis.

Young princes, the sons of concubines and of noble families, were educated together and formed early friendships. When they grew up they were favoured for loyalty and given honorary posts. Sometimes a princess might be given as wife to the son of a nobleman. The most important officials in the kingdom were bound together by education, friendship and blood.

According to the texts of the Old Kingdom there were some twenty provinces (which the Greeks called 'nomes') in Upper Egypt and a similar number in Lower Egypt. A governor ('nomarch'), the First Under the King, was appointed in each by royal decree. As a member of the ruling élite, the governor conducted his life in much the same manner as the aristocracy in the capital but on a smaller scale. He was the judge of the community and had complete control over all agricultural and public works. He supervised the census on cattle, produce and gold. He assessed taxes and controlled the archives where every local transaction, especially those involving land, were recorded. Taxes were assessed on the exact area of land irrigated. Warning of the approaching floods came from observers who

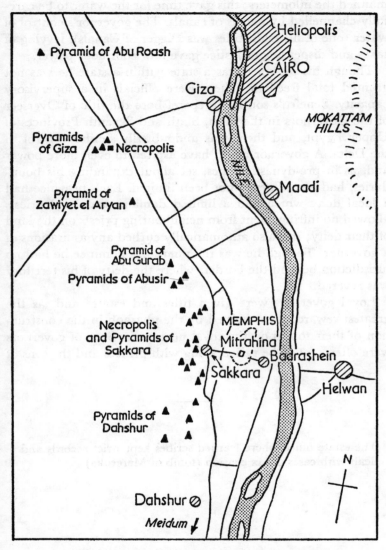

The burial grounds on the western bank of the Nile

manned the nilometers; this gave time for the water to be carefully channelled by means of canals. The governor's control of water (one of his main titles was Digger of Canals), levying of taxes and dispensing of justice gave him enormous power.

Though his province was a state within a state he was not granted total freedom. There were officials in a supervisory capacity. Senefru's son Netjereperef bore the title of Overseer of the Governors in the Fifth, Sixth and Seventh Provinces of Upper Egypt, and there was undoubtedly similar control in the Delta. A governor might have aspired to even more power and, as in pre-dynastic times, set about expanding his boundaries, had his influence not been limited. Each province had a local deity which had a limited domain, and local priests allowed no infringement from neighbouring priests on the land of their deity; this also automatically curbed any aspirations of a governor. Though he was the pharaoh's nominee he had no jurisdiction beyond the borders where the deity of his territory was revered.

Loyal governors were given titles and estates and, as the greatest reward, were assisted by the pharaoh in the construction of their tombs on the royal necropolis. Sons of governors were often sent to be raised along with princes and the sons of

---

The estate office where learned scribes kept strict records and dealt with cases of tax evasion (tomb of Mereruka)

noblemen in the capital. This was both an honour for the governor and an insurance against disloyalty for the pharaoh who permitted the post to become hereditary.

The administrative duties of a governor converged in the Chief Treasurer, and his judicial duties were organised in six courts under the Chief Justice of the Law; the Vizier was both Chief Treasurer and Chief Justice, and was therefore the link between the provinces and the central government. He was the mainspring of the government machinery, literally responsible for all the works of the king, 'the eyes and the ears of his sovereign . . . as a skipper, ever attentive (to his wants) both night and day'. He attended to every activity in the land, from the official counting of the country's assets, including arable land and cattle, to the assessment of taxes made on the inventories thus obtained. He was also the High Priest, with two assistants known as Treasurers of God. It was at one time thought that each pharaoh had only one Vizier, but evidence has come to light of two, sometimes many, holders of the title in a single reign. The wealth of the country was therefore controlled by a powerful religious body.

The Vizier's Hall in the palace was the archives of the state. Here the learned scribes with palette and reeds, ink cakes and

Shipbuilders (tomb of Ti)

papyrus rolls, kept full records, especially of taxpayers' names and the amounts they owed. Cursive writing, known as hieratic, became extensively used, especially for everyday government business. The more difficult hieroglyphic writing was reserved for religious texts. Dates were set by such inscriptions as the biennial cattle count: 'Year of Time 14 of the count of all oxen and small animals' (ie the 28th year of a king's reign). Though standard-weight rings of gold and copper were used in some palace transactions, coinage was unknown and taxes were calculated in produce: cattle, poultry, grain, wine and industrial products. These were stored in the granaries and storehouses. In instances of tax evasion officials with staves under their arms would not hesitate to 'sieze the town rulers for a reckoning'.

The learned scribes also drew up contracts and wills. The latter largely concerned the maintenance of tombs. Theoretically, of course, this was the responsibility of a man's heirs, but it was forseen that some laxity was to be expected with the passage of time. The testamentary endowments came from private property and in a man's will (literally 'order from his living mouth') he outlined that its income was to be put towards the care of his tomb and the continued supply of food and offerings considered essential for his afterlife. Mortuary priests were paid for these services. Hepzefi, a governor of Assiut, left no less than ten contracts elaborating his desires for the perpetual celebrations and maintenance of his tomb. In the case of royalty, the endowments were extremely large. Khafre's son, Nekure, bequeathed to his heirs a private fortune including fourteen towns and two estates at the royal residence, the entire income of which was for the maintenance of his tomb; and he made the will 'while he was alive upon his two feet without ailing in any way'.

The fact that no written law has been found in ancient Egypt does not undermine documentary evidence of legal practice. Written briefs were submitted to a governor, who frequently inscribed in his tomb that he 'judged two partners until they were satisfied'. Among the Old Kingdom legal evidence is a document referring to litigation between an heir and an executor. It indicated that under certain circumstances an appeal might be made directly to the central Court. There is one remarkable case of treason in the royal harem which was heard by two provincial judges (governors) in place of the Chief Judge (the Vizier), for an unbiased decision. Some were simple contracts such as the document known as 'The contract for the sale of a small house'. The most famous legal case was that of the Vizier Kheti, whose name lived on until the New Kingdom as 'the judge whose case was more than justice'. Kheti was involved in a lawsuit in which members of his own family were party; his judgement was against his own relative in order not to be accused of partiality. An appeal was made, yet Kheti persisted and his second ruling was the same as the first.

THE GOD-KING'S AUTHORITY

It is abundantly clear that the Heliopolis priests exercised a unique authority over the pharaohs of the Pyramid Age. Their tombs (see Chapter 6) were symbols of the sun cult. They were enlarged versions of the sacred *ben-ben* or mound at Heliopolis where Atum-Ra the Sun-god was believed to have manifested himself. The Vizier Hemeon, who built the Great Pyramid for the pharaoh Khufu (Cheops), was a 'devotee of Heliopolis'. And after Khufu's death four of his successors proclaimed their religious loyalties by forming their names of compounds of the Sun-god: Djede*fre*, Kha*fre* (Chephren), Bau*fre* and Menkau*re* (Mycerinius). The word 'pharaoh' did not mean 'King' in the Old Kingdom. References to the monarch were in such terms as 'Great House' (*Per-O* from which 'pharaoh' is derived) or 'Protected Place'. The term implied the palace and its connected halls and chambers which housed the government departments. Thus the Great House had complete authority, both secular and religious. The officials in the palace were not the docile instruments of a monarch's will but themselves vital cogs in the administrative wheel. The so-called absolute power of the pharaoh is only theoretical. Opinions have unfortunately been formed less on evidence than on the size and number of monuments. For instance, although the sole testimony to the autocratic power of Khufu (Cheops), builder of the Great Pyramid, is his tomb, his personal power has all too often been measured by its dimensions, overlooking the evidence that it was the Great House that exercised authority over the provinces, monopolised mining and marketing and supervised building projects. There was, to be sure, a hierarchial political structure and a hierarchial pantheon of gods, but the God-king who stood at the apex of both was the vehicle by which the priests of Heliopolis exercised control.

The local deities, it will be remembered, were borne in their shrines by the local priests to attend the Heb-Sed Festival. Each had been given an incentive to witness the reassertion of the king's sovereignty over the Two Lands and accept him as a god mightier than their own. The God-king returned the compliment. He not only visited the district priests and made offerings in the local shrines but took an active part in their temple construction. Inscriptions indicate that Khufu restored the temple of Hathor the cow-goddess at Dendera, embellished another at Bubastis where the cat-goddess was worshipped, and consecrated gold, silver and bronze statues to the shrine of Selket, the scorpion-goddess, Hapi the Nile-god, and other deities. The part played by the Memphite Drama in anthropomorphisation should not pass unremarked: once a priest had dressed up as a god, or at least spoken and acted for a god, it was natural for the people to imagine their own local deities as men. In some cases the human figure was surmounted by their ancient ensigns, whether bird or animal. In other cases even the head was human but distinguished by ears or horns.

In the reign of Khafre (Chephren), builder of the second pyramid, magnificent cult figures of the God-king were fashioned. They described an immutable power that does not belong to mortals. The significant advances in the quality of royal statuary were not without purpose. They gave a feeling of strength, and permanency and helped promote the cult of the God-king. Menkaure (Mycerinius), builder of the third, smallest, pyramid at Giza, was frequently sculpted as a member of a group. These were Triads composed of the goddess Hathor, the pharaoh and *different* local deities, both male and female, bearing the features of the queen. There must once have been as many of these Triads as there were important provinces, just as the number of shrines in Zoser's Heb-Sed Court probably equalled the number of local deities who attended the festival. Religion cemented political unity, giving an inviolable character to the political system. Where gods were friends, men were united.

THE PYRAMID TEXTS

Religion and politics being inseparable, some sections of the religious literature could be interpreted in a political light. The Pyramid Texts are a compendium of writings inscribed on the tomb walls of the Pyramid of Unas, the last pharaoh of the 5th dynasty, and also on those of four of his successors of the 6th dynasty. The oldest and least corrupt of the religious writings of ancient Egypt, known to be derived from even older originals, they were modified, enlarged versions of early mythology, religious hymns and oral tradition. They contain some 714 verses or 'utterances'. Some are spoken by the king (in announcing himself to the gods of heaven). Others are spoken by the priests (especially those involving mortuary spells and the resurrection texts which form a large body of the literature). A section itemises offerings of food, drink, clothing, perfume and other items for the hereafter. The main theme of the Pyramid Texts is the raising of the dead pharaoh to take his place among the gods of heaven. They have sometimes been called a magical bulwark against death, the implication being that, since they were written in tombs, they served no other purpose than magically to assist the deceased pharaoh to heaven. This is not so. They were undoubtedly preached by the priests not only during the burial of the pharaoh but on other occasions as well.

It should be emphasised that the ancient Egyptians recorded in their tombs aspects of their lives on earth that they wished to repeat in the afterlife. In Chapters 5 and 6 we see how a nobleman who possessed estates, servants and a loving family, recorded all in his tomb. He also registered his titles, honours and duties, in the belief that by so doing he would enjoy the same eternally. The pharaoh, although recognised as divine, and however unapproachable he may have appeared to the people of Egypt, was a mere mortal. When he died he too, it was believed, would rise and live again to repeat his experience on earth.

It will be remembered that during the Heb-Sed Festival there was a re-enactment of the coronation when the various gods of Upper and Lower Egypt gave their consent to the renewal of kingship and accepted the God-king as one who had greater power than their local deity. The Pyramid Texts clearly confirm this:

> *Behold, the king is at the head of the gods and is provided as a god . . . the gods do obeisance when meeting the king just as the gods do obeisance when meeting the rising of Ra when he ascends from the horizon. (U. 687)*

An incentive to attend the Heb-Sed Festival was the bestowing of gifts on the different priesthoods. In the Pyramid Texts the phrase 'a boon which the king gives' is repeated in many utterances. Some are more explicit:

> *O all you gods who shall cause this pyramid and this construction of the king to be fair and endure; you shall be effective, you shall be strong, you shall have souls, you shall have power, you shall be given . . . bread and beer, oxen and fowl, clothing and alabaster . . .*
> *(U. 599)*

As some of the utterances confirm political realities, let us view others, not as mortuary spells for the afterlife, but as records of what actually took place.

The utterance declaring that the gods (ie the local priests) should obey the pharaoh is most precise:

> *It is I who restored you,*
> *It is I who built you up,*
> *It is I who set you in order,*
> *And you shall do for me everything which I say to you,*
> *Wherever I go . . . (U. 587)*

The implication that the gods who obeyed would be strong, effective and powerful (U. 599) is offset by the warning:

> *If I be cursed, then will Atum be cursed;*
> *If I be reviled, then will Atum be reviled;*
> *If I be smitten, then will Atum be smitten;*
> *If I am hindered on this road, then will Atum be hindered,*
> *For I am Horus,*
> *I have come following my father.*
> *I have come following Osiris. (U. 310)*

Did the pharaoh similarly warn the priests on his journeys throughout the land? And if reviled, what then? The texts state that the risen pharaoh joined the other gods in heaven, 'that he may *destroy* (their) power and confer (their) powers, (U. 318). And 'worship him . . . whom he wishes to live will live. *Whom he wishes to die will die.*' (U. 217)

Was this a warning against extinction? According to Herodotus, Khufu (who restored the temple of Hathor, embellished one at Bubastis and consecrated precious ornaments to that of Selket) closed down the temples in the land in order to recruit slave labour to raise his monumental tomb. The Westcar Papyrus, a document relating events in the Old Kingdom, confirms that he did indeed order the closing down of at least one temple. A local deity without a temple would be absorbed by a neighbouring deity (who would acquire its chief characteristics and adopt some of its regalia or emblems), but its priests would cease to be effective. The sons of local priests appear to have succeeded their fathers in their calling, generation after generation, until they formed a sacerdotal nobility in each province. The possibility of being deprived of their means of livelihood, their temple, was too terrible to contemplate. In this context the following verse, spoken by the priests, is particularly relevant:

> *O King, may your soul stand among the gods and*
> *among the spirits, for it is* fear of you *which*
> *is on their hearts. O King, succeed to your throne*
> *at the head of the living, for it is* dread of you
> *which is in their hearts.* (*U. 422*)

Here, finally, we have textual endorsement that the God-king, who symbolised the collective power of the local gods—for 'he has swallowed the intelligence of every god. Lo, their souls are in the king's belly, their spirits are in the king's possession . . .' (U. 273/4) had complete control over them by instilling a sense of dread in the hearts of the local priests.

Many of the utterances were repeated time and again in different contexts, sometimes with only slight variation in meaning. The phrase 'Recite the words' also preceded some of the utterances and is sure indication of their purpose. They were current dogma. Through the power of repetition the people believed. The texts were recited not only on the day of burial but on other occasions as well, particularly during feasts in various parts of the country. It is clear that the priests who ordered their inscription had long circulated and preached their content.

The Heliopolis priests were not a dogmatic body of thinkers. They had formulated the first state religion, not by banner headlines announcing the supremacy of the Sun-god, but by carefully assessing the potential up and down the Nile valley, by delving into tradition and folklore and by trading on the popularity of sun worship. Well aware of the superstitions of the people, they subtly appropriated the popular beliefs of the different areas and modified them into a coherent tale. They undermined beliefs they considered irrelevant by denouncing them as enemies of the Sun-god, and embellished what they regarded pertinent. They superimposed the different interpretations of sun worship, one upon the other, like transparencies through which earlier and differing ideas could be discerned. Their doctrine was completely in the spirit of tradition.

In the Pyramid Texts only *On* (Heliopolis) is mentioned. Atum-Ra the Sun-god presides over the Great Ennead (U. 601). Ptah, the god of Memphis, is significant for his absence. The Heliopolis priests satisfied in one massive literary creation the paradoxical nature and solar beliefs; the single overwhelming theme that emerged was that in death the resurrected pharaoh became Osiris while his throne on earth was taken over by his son Horus; and that Horus, the God-king, who restored and built the settlements, had the authority both to destroy and to confer power.

THE HELIOPOLIS-MEMPHIS RIVALRY RENEWS

The political structure was based on a sound, but unfortunately not enduring, religious system. It could survive only so long as the cult of the God-king remained firm. By the reign of Menkaure (Mycerinius) there is indication of a weakening of the centralised government. It is significant, therefore, that in the Great House during his reign, and also during that of his successor Shepseskaf, there was a certain official named *Ptah-*Shepses. His name indicates that simultaneously with the loss of pharonic prestige a member of the palace was loyal to the priesthood of Memphis. Suddenly we have evidence that the hitherto inviolable ranks of the Heliopolis priests had been penetrated by the rival cult.

Menkaure probably met an untimely death, for he planned but never completed his Valley Temple. And Shepseskaf, who succeeded to the throne appears not to have been a son of 'The Great Royal Wife'; he was not of pure Heliopolitan blood. Shepseskaf digressed from the Heliopolis tradition in several other respects: he changed the shape of his tomb (in place of a pyramid, the symbol of the sun-cult, his 'Mastaba Fara'un' was shaped like a large rectangular sarcophagus), and it was not situated on the Giza plateau opposite Heliopolis, but on the Sakkara plateau nearer Memphis; and he failed to acknowledge, either in name or title, any connection with the cult of Ra.

One wonders what part *Ptah*-Shepses played in the above, especially since he married Shepseskaf's eldest daughter and forthwith declared himself High Priest of Ptah. This political marriage was bound to have far-reaching consequences.

The last pharaoh of the 4th dynasty compounded his name with the god of the Memphites. He was called Dede*ptah*. He reigned for only two years and after his death there is evidence that a compromise was reached between the priests of Heliopolis and Memphis, a division of power. The pharaohs were still of Heliopolitan descent as ascribed to them by popular tradition, but no longer was the pharaoh's eldest son the most important official in the land. The post of Chief Vizier-Judge became the prerogative of the Memphite families. Five of the 5th-dynasty viziers bear the name of Ptahhotep and were buried at Sakkara. It is from the tomb of one of them (an important official in the reign of the 5th-dynasty pharaoh Djedkare), and from the tombs of other 5th-dynasty noblemen, that we know most about how the ancient Egyptians lived (Chapter 5), worked (Chapter 6) and spent their leisure time (Chapter 7).

A text known as the Westcar Papyrus explains the continued predominance of the state cult of the Heliopolitan priesthood in the 5th dynasty. It contains a prophesy by a powerful sorcerer that Reddedet, the wife of a priest, would give birth to three sons by the Sun-god Ra. These children, he declared, were destined for the throne. The pharaoh would forthwith be physically as well as spiritually the 'son of the Sun-god'. With great enthusiasm the priests announced that the first three pharaohs of the 5th dynasty would be Reddedet's sons by immaculate conception and that the first would also be High

Priest of Heliopolis. Reddedet may be identified with Khant-kawes, whose tomb was found at Giza, and whose cult was assiduously kept throughout the 5th dynasty; she bore the title 'Mother of Two Kings'.

The Westcar Papyrus only appeared in written form some five centuries after the fall of the Old Kingdom. Since it largely related tales of magical feats it has been placed in the literary genre of popular stories transmitted by oral tradition. The text is, however, of historical value, for all the stories are set in the Old Kingdom and mention the names of kings and princes in chronological order. In the context of the increasing strength of the Memphite priests during the reigns of Menkaure and Shepseskaf, the Westcar Papyrus may in addition preserve the undercurrents of a most inspired, imaginative and successful campaign to boost the dwindling reputation of the Heliopolitan priests.

It was Khufu, builder of the great pyramid, who asked his sons to tell him tales of wonders. The first two magical feats they recounted took place in the reigns of the 3rd-dynasty pharaohs Zoser and Nebka. The third tale told of the magical power of a sorcerer in Senefru's reign and the fourth in Khufu's own reign. The tales end with the prophecy of the imminent birth of the three children of the Sun-god destined for the throne.

Wondrous tales for the credulous masses of how a sorcerer folded back the waters of a lake in order that a pharaoh, sailing with a maiden companion, could recover the jewel she had dropped; of how a sorcerer, on learning of his wife's deception, ordered his wax crocodile to carry off his rival; of how another, in Khufu's own reign, brought decapitated geese back to life, garnished and would assure widespread circulation for the prophecy of the divine births. The stories seem to have the decided flavour of a propaganda bid.

The success of the Heliopolis priests is attested by the fact that, in the 5th dynasty, it became an established custom to have royal names compounded with that of the Sun-god

(Sahu*re*, Neferirka*re*, Shepseska*re*, Neferef*re*, Nyuser*re*, etc) and a new epithet 'Son of Ra' became a regular concomitant, usually outside the cartouche. In addition, there is evidence on the Palermo Stone of abundant gifts of land and offerings to the Sun-god Ra and the 'Souls of *On*' (Heliopolis) in the 5th dynasty. Finally, a new monument, a Sun Temple, was constructed. These were different in design from anything hitherto built. They comprised a huge open court surrounded by a high wall, with the whole temple so oriented that the rising sun would

'Son of Ra' title

cast its rays through the entrance to the east and strike, at the opposite end of the court, a huge, squat obelisk resting on a mastaba-like base of hewn stone. The obelisk was patterned after the symbol of the Sun-god, being an elevated *ben-ben* stone, the sacred symbol of Heliopolis. The first Sun Temple was built in the reign of Sahure, the second of the three divine pharaohs, and five of his successors also built them.

The royal burial grounds move southwards to Abu Sir, between Giza (the necropolis of Heliopolis) and Sakkara (the necropolis of Memphis). As might be expected following the division of power, the pyramids of the pharaohs were of inferior workmanship and materials, with loose blocks and rubble at the core.

DECLINE OF THE OLD KINGDOM

Divine kingship did not remain frozen at its inception. When the political structure was strong, the God-king was strong. When wealth was depleted and loyalties divided, the God-king lost prestige. With the loss of prestige came loss of power. From generation to generation in the 4th dynasty, one family had headed the priesthood, nominated the governors, pronounced final judgement and reaped the benefits of a highly organised state. There was no overshadowing of their figurehead, the pharaoh. It was the God-king who smote enemies, conducted expeditions and attended official functions. The God-king was the symbol of power and the authority of the state. By the reign of Isesi, the fourth pharaoh of the 5th dynasty, we see the first hint of the rising power of the officials—a short text accompanying a relief of a triumphant march in which the officer in charge of the expedition is mentioned by name. The provincial governors began to agitate for independence. They were the first to throw off the restraint imposed by the Great House and establish themselves as landed lords.

According to the Annals of the Ramesside era, the direct line of Menes came to an end with Unas, the last pharaoh of the 5th dynasty, and a new dynasty of Memphite origin began.

The enfeebled monarchy proved powerless against the growing influence of the provincial governors. As power passed to them their local deities grew proportionately popular and sun worship was correspondingly on the wane. Among the fine reliefs in the Sun Temples is a representation of the pharaoh, once the 'Great Power, who has power over the powers . . . the most sacred of the sacred images of the Great One' (U. 273/4) depicted being nursed at the breast of the vulture-goddess of Nekhen. This revealing vision of the God-king's power being so reduced that he takes sustenance from another god is followed by further loss of prestige: by the reign of the 6th dynasty pharaoh Pepi I he is kneeling before another god to present offerings. And finally, among the ruins of the causeway of Pepi II's pyramid, we see him no longer as a God-king, but represented as a sphinx and a griffin, trampling enemies.

There were violent political disturbances during the transition from the 5th to 6th dynasties. The governors abandoned their title 'First after the King' and called themselves 'Great

Chief' (Lord) with the name of their province. One Great Chief boasted of bringing people from neighbouring areas to settle in the outlying districts of his province to infuse new blood into it. No longer aspiring to be buried on the royal necropolis, in the shadow of their pharaoh's pyramid, the Great Chiefs constructed tombs in their own provinces.

The country had segmented into those very provinces of Upper and Lower Egypt which had emerged from the strongest neolithic settlements. At the end of the 6th dynasty political confusion erupted in national chaos. Civil war broke out and the monarchy collapsed.

Many factors probably contributed to the collapse of the Old Kingdom. It may have been the undertaking of huge non-economic enterprises like the building of the Great Pyramids. The royal house may have been impoverished by maintaining temples whose endowments increased from generation to generation. The famine of the 5th dynasty may have hastened its collapse (in the causeway of the pyramid of Unas are scenes showing men with bony limbs and hollow flanks sucking their fingers to appease the pains of hunger), or the need to fight aggression (the first battle scenes appear in Sahure's Sun Temple). Or it may have been the division of power and wealth between two opposing factions, following the first crack in the structure when *Ptah*-Shepses infiltrated the Heliopolitan ranks, married a pharaoh's daughter and became High Priest of Ptah. The final rift may, indeed, have come when Pepi I married a woman of non-royal blood and, in breaking the class structure, shattered the very foundations upon which the Old Kingdom rested. Political rivalry between two priesthoods, which fired the cultural explosion in the Old Kingdom, seems also to have been a main cause for its collapse.

RIVAL CULTS

Strangely enough it is from the verbal tradition that survived until the classical author Herodotus came to Egypt that we find considerable support for the hypothesis of rival cults. According to tradition the three pharaohs Khufu (Cheops), Dedefre and Khafre (Chephren), who ruled a stable and unified country, were all tyrants who 'plunged into all kinds of wickedness'. Khufu was described as a megalomaniac; he reputedly sent his daughter to procure money for him, charging visitors a sum equivalent to a finished limestone block for her favours.

Why did these pharaohs, revered during their lifetime, suffer so slanderous an attack after their deaths? Were the allegations of years of tyranny so much political backbiting? Was Khufu the prototype of the political scapegoat, and his closing of a few temples exaggerated into the closing of 'all the temples of the land'? Was the recruiting of labour during the months of the inundation when work was at a standstill anyway, and when the Great House housed and fed the otherwise idle farmers in pyramid towns (Chapter 5), reinterpreted as tyranny? Or was it a partisan exercise by the Memphites to blacken the image of their rivals? If so, it seems they took credit for the good their rivals accomplished: in the mortuary temple of the 5th-dynasty pharaoh Sahure, the second of the divine sons of Reddedet, there is a mural showing Libyan nobility being brought as prisoners. The text specifies the names of the Libyan princes and the number of cattle taken as booty. This scene is repeated in the mortuary temple of Pepi II of the 6th dynasty, the twelfth pharaoh after Sahure, when Memphite influence was re-established. The Libyan princes bear exactly the same names, and exactly the same number of cattle are recorded!

Menkaure (Mycerinius), according to Herodotus, reopened the temples and allowed the people to return to their shrines. He was said to be 'fair and just' and compensated the poor. But calamity fell upon him. First his daughter, an only child, died and 'the gods decided' that he would only reign for six years upon the earth and that in the seventh 'thou shalt end thy days'. The angered Menkaure asked why it was that his father and uncle 'though they shut the temples, took no thought of the gods and destroyed multitudes of men, nevertheless enjoyed a long life [while] . . . I, who am pious, am to be doomed?' Why indeed? Could it have been because Menkaure, despite the influence of Ptah-shepses, was nevertheless of pure Heliopolitan descent?

THE OLD KINGDOM'S INFLUENCE

Egypt's youth was also the peak of its maturity. The rules that governed the Old Kingdom were never to govern again. The conditions that gave rise to the centralised state no longer existed. In a changed society, new concepts took shape and gave rise to new ideals. So deeply rooted, however, were the traditions established during the period from the unification of the Two Lands by Narmer until the first social revolution after the fall of the 6th dynasty that even when the masses attacked the institutions of Egypt they could not destroy their essential character. The Old Kingdom continued to influence political and social patterns, philosophy and artistic processes for another 2,000 years, until the Greek conquest.

4

How They Travelled

INTERNAL MOVEMENT

THERE was ceaseless activity in ancient Egypt. Grain and industrial products were brought to the capital from the provinces of Upper and Lower Egypt. Journeys were made from village to village and to and from oases for commercial exchange. Excursions were organised to distant areas in search of raw materials. Pilgrimages were regularly made to the shrines of important deities. And from the settlements in the valley to the burial grounds on the desert plateau the people bore their dead for burial, or offerings to place at the shrines of departed friends and relatives.

In the rural areas the people travelled on foot, and donkeys were the most common beasts of burden. As they made their way to the granaries and storehouses, laden with produce, their routes were trodden into firm dirt-track roads. These were used by the peasant community, by herdsmen and their cattle, by female offering-bearers from the estates, and as playgrounds for children.

Almost the whole of the cultivable soil of Egypt was used for crop-growing and the land was irrigated through a system of large and small canals. The farmer who dug a canal to regulate the flow of water to his crops simultaneously constructed a dyke with the excavated earth, and this served as a path between the fields. Since regular attention was given to canals to guide water to land that would otherwise remain barren, and

E
69

precautions were intermittently taken to prevent overflooding, the paths were kept in good order, and were used by the farmers and their livestock. Larger dykes beside deep canals could serve also as towpaths for small boats. There were no bridges: when a canal had to be crossed a herdsman simply guided his animals through the shallow water.

A provincial nobleman was borne around his estates in a carrying-chair on the shoulders of pole-bearers. From this vantage he could inspect granaries, fisheries and agricultural lands. With his chair placed on the ground at his destination, he could watch in comfort the progress being made in the glass-making, copper, leather and papyrus factories, in carpentry shops, ateliers and the shipyard.

The Nile, the vital artery that linked Upper and Lower Egypt and contributed to national unity, since it made all parts of the land easily accessible, was the main means of communication. When the pharaoh carried out his annual tour of inspection, known as the 'Following of Horus', he travelled the watery highway in his royal barge. It was the most practical method of transporting crops and industrial products destined for the royal treasury and of transporting giant monoliths from distant quarries to the necropolis.

There were many different types of vessel, ranging from royal barges to ocean-going vessels and papyrus craft for hunting and fishing on the Nile. The ships in which noblemen and officials travelled had deck-houses and single sails, and were usually steered by rudders shaped like oars. The cargo vessels, with the goods placed on deck, sometimes transported granite blocks weighing hundreds of tons. Boats travelling northwards were helped by the current, those southbound by the prevailing north wind: Nile traffic was facilitated by natural conditions. Since waterways were the main means of communication it is interesting to observe that the ancient Egyptians regarded the ferrying of a boatless traveller across a canal or marshy area as a good deed, of the calibre of giving food to the hungry and clothing to the poor.

No effort was spared to build the most beautiful and enduring monuments and no distance was too great to travel in
search of wood, metal and stone of the finest quality. The extent
of internal movement and communication can best be realised
by considering the widely separated areas from which the raw
material came. Copper and turquoise from the mines in Sinai;
basalt from the eastern delta, limestone from the Mokattam
Hills near Cairo; alabaster came from Hat-Nub in Middle
Egypt, fine-quality granite from the quarries of Aswan near
Egypt's southern border; and the diorite quarries were in the
western desert of Lower Nubia.

Sarcophagi and statues were roughly shaped before transportation in order to reduce the weight, and the method of
transportation is graphically depicted in a Middle Kingdom
representation of a colossal seated statue, 22ft high, being
towed by 172 men in four double lines. As they drag the
securely bound statue with ropes, a man pours water in front
of the sledge to ease the friction. In a New Kingdom representation in Hatshepsut's Mortuary Temple, two obelisks
are being transported by river. We have no such representations
dating to the Old Kingdom but can assume that stone was
similarly transported. The blocks were probably eased on to
wooden sledges and towed by gangs of men to the river; they
would then be levered on to barges and, having sailed to their
destination on the swift-flowing currents during the inundation, would again be transferred to sledges, for dragging to the
necropolis. Although there is a representation of a scaling-
ladder on wheels in a 5th-dynasty tomb, wheels were not used
for transportation in the Old Kingdom.

It is not surprising that a powerful and cultured state should
conserve its natural wealth and seek to augment supplies from
regions around it, as well as seek out materials not available
within its borders. One such region lay beyond the First
Cataract in the south, and was a difficult area to reach. At low
water the river Nile struggled through a six-mile course of
sinuous, tortuous passages dividing round rocks, dashing over

protusions and fermenting and gurgling its way northward.
During the inundation the danger would be under water, but
the turbulent eddies betrayed the presence of the bed of reefs.
Beyond lay Nubia.

TRAVEL IN NUBIA

Egyptian incursions into Nubia, a land rich in copper and
gold ores, started from early times. Djer, the 1st-dynasty
pharaoh, left an inscription at the entrance to the Second
Cataract depicting several corpses and a man being taken as
prisoner (probably no more than a punitive raid), and there is
evidence that one site in Nubia near a particularly rich vein of
copper was occupied for two centuries for the smelting of large
quantities of ore. By the 4th and 5th dynasties there was
considerable activity there. Rock inscriptions at Kulb, a gold-
mining area, indicate the most southern point at which Old
Kingdom prospectors worked.

Exploitation of Nubia's mineral wealth does not imply
colonisation which did not, in fact, occur until the Middle
Kingdom (when massive fortresses were constructed at the
Second Cataract). The expeditions, though primarily conducted to satisfy Egyptian requirements, were mutually
beneficial. Egypt acquired highly valued commodities including gold, myrrh, electrum (a gold and silver alloy), ebony,
animal skins (especially panther) and gums, and the Nubians
depended on Egypt for corn, oil, honey, clothing and other
items. The Nile in Nubia was flanked by a wall of hills to east
and west which closely confined the valley, and apart from the
narrow strip between the river and the ridges, the land was
desolate, the Nubians impoverished. They lived in squalid low-
built houses in settlements along the river's edge or beside water
holes and channels.

It was from the Nubian tribes that a 6th-dynasty nobleman
called Uni recruited troops to suppress agitating Bedouins in
the frontier provinces of the Delta, in order to safeguard
Egyptian sources of raw material in Sinai. Egypt had no

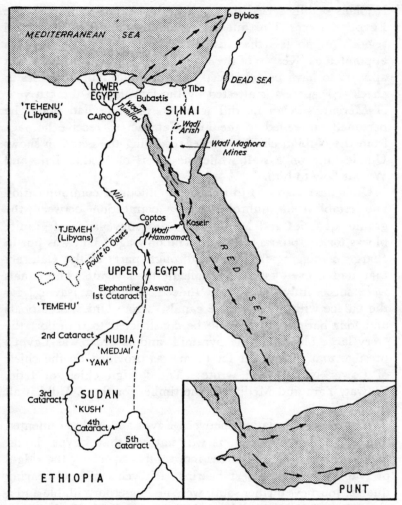

Ancient names and travel routes to Nubia, Punt and Asia

standing army at this time, and there is little doubt that the Nubians readily seized the opportunity of finding work in the Egyptian forces. Uni quelled revolts in the Delta and Sinai regions on no less than five occasions and was thenceforth appointed as 'Keeper of the Door of the South'. His main task appears to have been to keep the bordering Nubian tribes in check. His success is attested by the fact that in the 5th year of Merenre's reign he did what no pharaoh had done: he personally travelled to the First Cataract to receive homage from the Nubian chiefs. A relief recording the occasion shows Uni leaning on a staff while the chiefs of Medja, Irtje and Wawat bow to him.

Uni's next task was to improve methods of communication and establish an unbroken water connection between the granite quarries and Memphis, to aid conveyance of granite blocks for the pharaoh's tomb. The now-aged Uni was put in charge of digging five canals through parts of the Cataract that had proved especially difficult to navigate. The canals were successfully excavated; 'Indeed, I made a [saving] for the palace with all these five canals,' wrote Uni. Three boats and four barges had then to be constructed to transport the 'very large blocks for the pyramid' and so great was Egypt's prestige that the timber for them was provided by the chiefs of Lower Nubia. Uni wrote: 'The foreign chiefs of Irtje, Wawat, Yam and Medja cut the timber for them. I did it all in one year.'

With peaceful relations between Egypt and Nubia cemented and the waterway open, it was natural that Egypt should exploit the surrounding areas more fully, especially the ridges of Nubia's eastern desert bearing rich veins of gold-bearing quartz. Journeys further south were no longer formidable and a closer interest in Yam (Upper Nubia) and Kush (Sudan) was also inevitable. The tombs of successive noblemen clearly indicate the vigorous approach being introduced in Egypt's foreign policy towards the end of the Old Kingdom. 'Caravan-leaders', travelling on foot accompanied by pack-donkeys, began to venture further south and explore hitherto unknown regions of Africa.

Harkhuf, a powerful nobleman and caravan-leader from Elephantine was the first recorded explorer in history. He made four journeys to Yam, the inhospitable country south of the Second Cataract, and also travelled westwards to un-explored regions on the 'Elephant Road', which may have been the route extending southwards from Aswan which is still used today for transporting herds from the Sudan. His first journey took seven months. His second was more adventurous and he recorded that 'never had any companion or caravan-leader who went forth to Yam done (it)', and also that he brought back items 'the likes of which no one has ever brought back before'. When Harkhuf reached Yam on his third expedition he found the country in an uproar. The chiefs were engaged in war with the settlements of Temehu (tribes related to the Libyans). Egypt had always acted on the defensive against incursions on the Nile valley from the western desert. Under the adventurous Harkhuf, however, a convoy followed the chief of Yam west-wards and reduced him to subjection. On his return journey Harkhuf's convoy, laden with tributes and products and fur-nished with a heavy escort, so impressed the tribal chiefs of the Nubian border that, instead of plundering the convoy, they offered Harkhuf guides and cattle. It was on his fourth journey that Harkhuf brought back to Egypt gold, ostrich feathers, lion and leopard skins, elephant tusks, cowrie shells, logs of ebony, incense, gum arabic and a dancing pygmy (Chapter 7).

The foot convoys into the unknown interior must have been interminable and exhausting. Accompanied by pack-donkeys the caravan-leaders were obliged to travel very slowly, follow-ing old river channels where wells and springs could be found. It took months to cover routes that camels can today cover in a few weeks. The expeditions were usually successful, but they were not without hazard and more than one nobleman lost his life venturing into the interior.

The Egyptians were well acquainted with some of the languages and dialects of the tribes of Nubia, and the loose sovereignty they exercised over them was respected; the Nubians had long been won over by admiration. A more aggressive policy towards them only becomes apparent towards the close of the Old Kingdom, and the complete conquest of Lower Nubia occurred in the Middle Kingdom.

Egypt commanded the routes to the south. Broken pottery vessels bearing the names of the pharaohs Pepi I, Merenre and Pepi II have been found as far south as Kerma in the Sudan. The gateway to the vast riches of interior Africa was open. Caravans could explore overland routes to distant Punt on the Somali Coast, an area rich in incense, ointments, and other exotica considered indispensable to the wealthy.

SEA VOYAGES

Egyptian ships sailed across the Mediterranean Sea (the 'Great Green') from earliest times, and also down the Red Sea to the remote waters of Punt, and the southern side of the Gulf of Aden. They were sea worthy vessels with long hull, high curved stern with two rudders situated on each side of it, a single mast held by four ropes and a wide sail—not much different from river craft but modified for added stresses. The Egyptian fleet was a familiar sight at Byblos, on the Phoenician coast. Cedar grew abundantly on the wooded slopes of Lebanon and there was an active exchange of Egyptian products for timber, particularly, and other items of the east.

So strong was Egyptian influence on the Phoenician coast that an Egyptian temple was erected in Byblos in the 4th dynasty and many objects inscribed with the names of pharaohs have been found in both town and harbour areas. In Sahure's Sun Temple a relief depicts the timber fleet returning to Egypt with Semitic-Syrians aboard, their arms uplifted in homage to the pharaoh. Sahure also sent ships to Punt and, indeed, navigation down the Red Sea was more frequent than is usually supposed.

As no waterway linked the Nile and the Red Sea, ships were constructed in the Delta, usually on the easterly branch of the river near Bubastis, where vessels of shallow draught could be towed during the inundation through the Wadi Tumilat towards the Eastern Marshes. It was whilst engaged in building a ship in the Delta that a caravan-leader and the troop with him were murdered by Bedouin tribes. Pepi-Nakht, a competent nobleman, was sent for all the way from Elephantine to resolve the problem and recover the body.

Some vessels may have sailed on a direct route between Byblos and Punt, a journey that would have required them to navigate southwards through the most easterly branch of the Nile towards Bubastis, through the Wadi Tumilat to the Eastern Marshes and thence southwards through the Gulf of Suez to the Red Sea. A 'Byblos ship' meant a seaworthy vessel. On the western shore of the Red Sea they would pick up foot convoys which had made their way from Elephantine to Coptos (the point where the Nile most closely approaches the Red Sea), and thence through the dried-out river bed of the Wadi Hammamat (where mineral mines were located) to the coast to join the southward-bound vessels. The frequency of expeditions to Punt is apparent from the tomb text of a subordinate official from Elephantine, who recorded that he accompanied his lord on a dozen occasions. The imports from one journey alone were 80,000 measures of myrrh, some 6,000 weight of electrum and 2,600 staves of ebony.

TRAVEL IN ASIA

On the outer wall of his Sun Temple, Sahure is depicted triumphing over Libyans on the south side and Asiatics on the north side. These were 'sand-dwellers', nomads of Libyan and Semitic origin. Those to the east, in Sinai, lived chiefly upon the milk of their flocks of goats and sheep. Though some groups settled around springs where they tilled the soil, their existence was precarious. They had to supplement their provisions from

Egypt and not surprisingly the sight of the riches in the north-eastern Delta awoke in them an instinct to pillage. There are records of incursions into Egyptian territory from early times. Towards the end of the 5th dynasty and during the 6th they had become particularly bold and were continually raiding the Egyptians in the eastern Delta as well as in Wadi Maghera mines in Sinai.

It was to quell these revolts that Uni had recruited Nubian tribes into a fighting force. After scattering the enemy he gathered his untrained troops on the frontier at the 'Isle of the North' (probably somewhere in the region of Ismailia) and set out into the desert. He advanced as far as Wadi Arish where the southern tribes finally submitted. Those to the north of Sinai, however, whose seaboard was the Mediterranean, threatened to dispute Egypt for possession of the land, and Uni decided to attack them from the sea. The Egyptian fleet carried his forces to Tiba, to the north of Wadi Arish, and after a successful campaign Egypt continued to work the mineral mines in Sinai without threat.

Having established Egyptian control of Sinai, Uni led incursions into the populous areas near the south of the Dead Sea where his now-experienced contingent quelled a revolt on the coast of southern Palestine, beating the enemy to the highlands of Palestine, the most northern point to which the pharaohs of the Old Kingdom advanced.

As a result of the newly born power of the noblemen, Egyptian influence in Asia might have continued, had the country not been torn by the internal problems that caused the collapse of the Old Kingdom. Particularly interesting, however, is the totally unwarlike spirit at that time. Though the Egyptians looked with contempt on the 'sand-dwellers' and the 'barbarians' who were their neighbours, Uni's autobiography text, typical of the period, rings more of pride in a mission successfully accomplished than of aggression.

5

How They Lived

ENJOYMENT OF LIFE

MOST of the buildings of ancient Egypt, including the royal palace, were built of wood and brick. Stone was reserved for tombs and temples, and most of the surviving structures are therefore of a funerary nature, which gives the erroneous impression that the ancient Egyptians were preoccupied with thoughts of the afterlife. Evidence to the contrary is abundant. The ancient Egyptians thought of the afterlife simply as an inevitable extension of their earthly experience, and decorated their tombs with aspects of their lives they wished to repeat. These graphic murals in fact provide clear indication of how conscientiously they channelled their energies to the service of the living and to achieving comfort and pleasure on earth. Since our knowledge of life in ancient Egypt is chiefly derived from the murals and contents of the tombs of the wealthy official classes, we begin by reviewing their lives, afterwards discussing the working classes and the royal family.

THE NOBLEMEN

Three of the most famous and well-preserved tombs of the Old Kingdom are situated at Sakkara. They belong to Ti (Supervisor of Works, Scribe of the Court and Royal Counsellor under three pharaohs of the 5th dynasty), Ptahhotep (one of the highest officials in the land in the reign of Djedkare in

79

the 5th dynasty) and Mereruka, the son-in-law of the 6th-dynasty pharaoh Teti. These tombs, and others of the same period, provide a rich saga of the daily lives of the nobles' families.

A man's tomb was constructed on the pattern of a house. Unlike the tomb, however, houses were light structures, usually of sun-dried brick and wood. They were airy and well suited to the warm climate with latticed windows and large open courtyards. Every householder had a garden and gardening came to play a large part in the daily lives of the wealthy families. Vines, palms, fruit and vegetables grew on their estates. The fact that the ancient Egyptians were great nature-lovers is attested by the encyclopedic lists of birds, plants and animals recorded in national monuments.

All their useful items were beautiful and they took an obvious pride in their possessions. Chairs and beds (which often had leather or rope-weave seats or mattresses fastened to the frame with leather throngs) had legs carved in the form of the powerful hind-limbs of ox or lion; furniture frequently had decorative copper fittings. The handle of a spoon might be fashioned to resemble a lotus blossom, or the calyx might form the bowl of a wine glass. As early as the 1st dynasty a stone lamp was shaped like a papyrus bud with a horizontal groove for the wick; by the 5th dynasty lamps were elegantly fashioned with a large bowl and set on a stand. Chests and boxes were richly inlaid with ivory. Vases and vessels of copper, gold and silver were equipped with stands to raise them to the required height. Tables were either round on a central pedestal or shaped like a half-oblong on four legs. Both beds and chairs tended to be low, the occupant of the latter having to recline or squat, and guests sometimes sat on mats on the floor. The walls were decorated like hanging mats and the ceilings were often painted blue.

Representations of tables laden with large varieties of food and drink show that the wealthy classes ate heartily. Confirmation comes from a tomb at Sakkara belonging to a lady of the

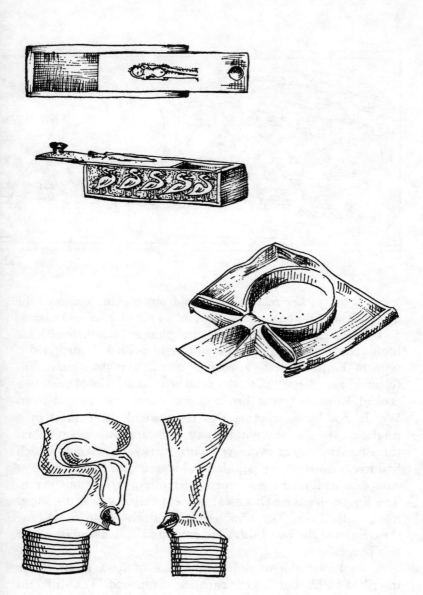

(*Top*): Carved pre-dynastic ivory box; (*Centre*): Early dynastic slate dish of two hieroglyph symbols; (*Bottom*): Legs of a bed

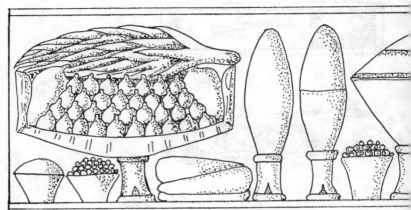

lesser nobility; her relatives had laid out a complete meal for her on rough pottery, alabaster and diorite bowls and dishes, and it was found beside her sarcophagus. Undisturbed for thousands of years, the food could be identified. It included a type of barley cereal, a cooked quail, a pigeon stew, fish (cleaned and dressed with the head removed), ribs of beef, two cooked kidneys, wheat bread, small cakes and stewed fruit. We do not know whether this represented the courses of a single meal. The Pyramid Texts indicate that people had three meals a day as compared with the royal household which had five. Fish was very popular and it seems that no larder was complete without its assortment of mullet, catfish and perch. The Egyptian caviar (*Botarikh*), a great delicacy, was produced from early times. The tombs of Ti and Kagemni show how the ovaries of the bouri fish were extracted, salted and dried for this purpose.

A wealthy nobleman drew up lists of food items to be inscribed in his tomb. One such list comprised 'Ten different kinds of meat, five kinds of poultry, sixteen kinds of bread and cakes, six kinds of wine, four kinds of beer, eleven kinds of fruit, in addition to all sorts of sweets and many other good

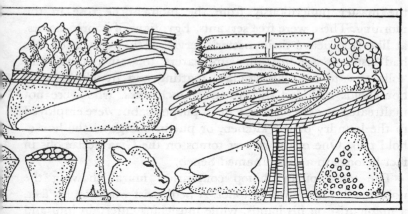

ings

things . . .' Beer, the national drink, was made from barley or wheat, sweetened with dates if desired, and stored in pottery jars. Wine was also produced from very early times.

All rich landowners possessed monkeys, gazelle, ibex and other animals of the desert which they caught, tamed and kept on their estates. They had long learned that the dog was man's best friend as well as his hunting companion, sheepdogs, greyhounds (often on a leash) and salukis were favourites. Greyhounds and salukis were allowed to enter the house or even sleep beneath the master's chair. There are no representations of a nobleman petting a dog, but the tomb of Kagemni has a relief of him watching a puppy being fed. Dogs were given names: one was buried near his master in a 1st-dynasty burial ground and his tombstone was inscribed 'Neb' (Lord), with his picture. Cats seem not to have been allowed in houses in the Old Kingdom, they were depicted only in papyrus groves, raiding birds' nests. The Nile goose was given special treatment, being allowed into courtyard and garden. Domestic fowl did not include cocks and hens, only ducks, pigeons, geese and waterfowl.

Wealthy households included numerous servants, attending

83

the master punctiliously from the moment he rose in the morning. These were free servants, Egyptians of poorer classes, at liberty to leave their master's service if they so wished. He had 'listeners' for his call, 'cup-bearers' to wait at table, and 'followers' to bear his sandals, matting and fly-whisk. Most households included dwarfs and hunchbacks, who were not maltreated or used for amusement purposes, but were employed in the laundry or the kitchen, or put in charge of the household pets. One of the richest tombs on the Giza necropolis in fact belongs to a dwarf named Seneb.

The tomb of Ptahhotep contains a mural showing the nobleman at his morning toilet. A pedicurist works on his feet, a manicurist on his hands, while musicians entertain him and his pet greyhound and a monkey take refuge beneath his chair. People were fastidious about cleanliness, especially the women. They took great pains with their toilet, washing their bodies with particular attention before meals, using a basin and a vessel with a spout. They shaved their limbs with bronze hooked razors with curved blades, and used tweezers and scrapers. Special care was taken with their hair, which they washed, anointed with oils and fashioned into curls and plaits with the aid of combs of wood and ivory. Women applied their

---

Agricultural scenes in naturalistic detail. Ploughing and milking are shown at the top, feeding stock and harvesting below

84

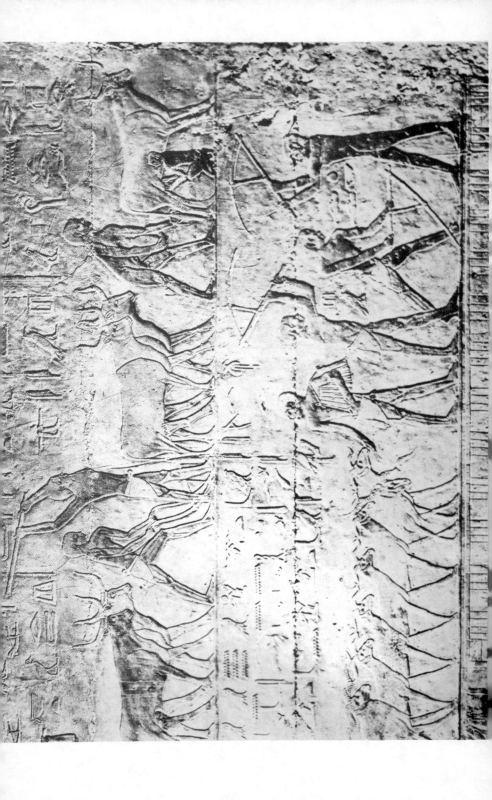

characteristic band of colour round the eye with a paint produced from lead ores and known from pre-dynastic times as a remedy for eye ailments as well as for adornment, using tiny ivory and wooden sticks and mirrors (polished metal discs with a handle). All small items were kept in decorative boxes of ebony, alabaster, marble and crystal, sometimes engraved with miniature bas-reliefs.

In a land of almost constant sunshine much clothing was unnecessary. Most garments were made of linen. Silk and cotton were unknown and wool only rarely used. The women wore a sheath from beneath the arms extending to the ankles with broad bands over the shoulders. The men wore short, broad, pleated skirts and sandals. Children, as befitted the climate, were left without clothing. Egyptians were not self-conscious about nudity. Maidservants and dancers had loincloths and girdles only, often with blossoms around the neck. The simple effect of the clothing was enhanced by colourful jewellery which both men and women loved to wear: elaborate coloured necklaces and bead collars, and bracelets for the women. Since the men usually kept their hair closely cropped, wigs were an important article of apparel among the upper classes.

The ancient Egyptians controlled insect pests by washing

Outdoor pursuits shown in the tomb of Ptahhotep. At the top, youths are wrestling; below this, pet greyhounds are being walked; at the bottom, hunters survey the spoils of the chase their houses with a solution of natron, and appear to have had well-developed drainage systems. In the mortuary temple of the 5th-dynasty pharaoh Sahure, this consisted of a stone tray-like basin in the base of which was a metal plug on a chain leading to a subterranean copper pipe. The drainage pipe, placed at an angle for the water to flow downwards, extended

The ancient Egyptians took great pains to wash and anoint their bodies. Ewers and basins depicted in a 6th-dynasty tomb

the whole length of the causeway, some 330 yards. The temple had several such basins, probably for personal washing.

A nobleman had one legal wife who was always Mistress of the House. A wealthy landowner might have concubines, but his wife held a special position and was treated with the utmost deference, and his heirs were her offspring. She shared with him not only his social life but inspections of his estate. In some reliefs a wife is seen clasping her husband round the waist or intimately sharing a repast with him. There was an obvious tenderness in family relations. No marriage contracts are known to exist, not is there any indication of a special ceremony. The marriage probably consisted of the actual transfer of the bride, together with her dowry, to the house of her appointed or approved husband, where his duties towards her are clear: 'If thou art a successful man establish thy household. Love thy wife in the house as is fitting . . . fill her body, clothe her back . . . the recipe for her limbs is ointment. Gladden her heart so long as she liveth . . . she is a profitable field for her lord.' These are the words of Ptahhotep, sage of the

5th dynasty, who was well advanced in years when he asked his pharaoh whether he could instruct his own son and prepare him for the official duties that lay ahead of him. The king consented and the aged vizier, wise from experience and learning, wrote some forty-three paragraphs of random instructions which have come down to us in four copies; three on papyrus and one on a wooden tablet. Half of them covered official duties and conduct in administrative circles (see Chapter 6). The other half covered personal character, conduct within the family, the duties of a son towards his father and mother and his behaviour towards friends and neighbours. The first piece of advice Ptahhotep gave to his son was on modesty: 'Be not proud because of thy learning. Take council with the unlearned as with the learned, for the limit of a craft is not fixed and there is no craftsman whose worth is perfect. Worthy speech is more hidden than a greenstone being found among slave-women at the mill-stone.'

Family relationships and good character were considered of vital importance. The father was the chief authority in a strictly disciplined home. 'Precious to a man is the virtue of his son, and good character is a thing remembered . . . if thou hearkenest to this which I have said to thee, all the fashion of thee will be according to the ancestors. As for the righteousness thereof, it is their worth . . . it shall not vanish from the mouths of men, because their maxims are worthy. Every word will be carried on; it shall not perish in this land forever . . .'

Tomb inscriptions indicate that youths had great respect for their fathers, and no effort was spared by a loyal son to ensure proper burial for his departed father. The case of Sebni comes to mind. His father was an official in charge of the Southern Gate (near the First Cataract), who was killed while venturing southwards on a trading mission. Sebni unhesitatingly set forth on the same journey in order to recover his father's body and bring it back to his native land for embalming and burial. Sebni's tomb at Aswan proudly records his loyal mission. One of the most frequent phrases of piety inscribed in tombs of this period was: 'I was one beloved of his father, praised of his mother, whom his brothers and sisters loved.'

The ancient Egyptians were discreet on matters of sexual behaviour, and immorality was strongly condemned: 'Beware,' warned Ptahhotep, 'of a woman from abroad, who is not known in her city. Look not upon her when she comes and know her not . . . If thou desirest to establish friendship in a house into which thou enterest . . . beware of approaching women. The place where they are is not seemly and it is not wise to intrude upon them. A thousand men are undone for the enjoyment of a brief moment like a dream . . .'

Concubines were placed in a special category and Ptahhotep told his son that they should be kindly treated; he also warned his son not to have any physical association with boys. As a solution to immorality, early marriages were recommended: a youth was advised to 'take to himself a wife when he is young that she might give him a son whom he will see a man. Happy is the man who has a large household and who is respected on account of his children.' Marriages between brothers and sisters were widespread among the pharaohs of the New Kingdom, during the Persian period, among the Ptolemies, and during the Roman occupation. There is, however, no confirmed disclosure of marriage between two children of the same parents in the Old Kingdom. The terms 'brother' and 'sister' were terms of endearment, and even after marriage a husband continued to call his wife *sonit* (sister), meaning 'loved one'. Unfortunately ancient Egyptian morality is often judged today by notorious practices found during the later periods of ancient Egyptian history: the Greeks declared that marriages between brothers and sisters were normal practice. However, Cambyses was told by the priests of Egypt that no law permitted it though a pharaoh could do as he wished.

Ptahhotep contrasted the good man with the bad, the wise man with the fool. He balanced desirable behaviour—characterised by moderation, reserve, discretion and gentleness—against the dangers of undesirable behaviour: excessive pride, boastfulness and avarice. Knowledge and advice was passed from father to son:

Greater is the appeal of the gentle than that of the strong.

Never utter words in heat. Let thy mind be deep and thy speech scanty.

The wise man rises early to establish himself, but the fool is in trouble.

When you sit with a glutton eat when his greed has passed; When you drink with a drunkard take when his heart is content.

Report on a thing observed, not heard.

Human relations were regarded as among a man's most valuable possessions. Ptahhotep stressed the togetherness of a husband and wife, the closeness of brothers and sisters. The basic unit of society was the family. In this context the pictorial reliefs take on new meaning. In the tomb of Mereruka, for example, are several scenes showing family devotion. One is an intimate and delightful bedroom scene with Mereruka and his wife watching their bed being prepared. In another he watches her as she sits on a large couch playing a harp. Family outings were encouraged: in Mereruka's tomb he can be seen affectionately holding his son by the hand (the boy holds a hoopoe bird in the other hand), and behind them are his wife and a row of attendants. In Ti's tomb he is depicted with his wife and daughter sailing through the marshes in a papyrus boat. This is the earliest chapter of family life in the history of man. There was no 'Book' or priestly instruction on morality and ethics. Right and wrong was a civil question, not a religious one.

From the earliest times the sacred rules of behaviour were based on an intuitive sense of what was agreeable and therefore right, and what was unacceptable and therefore wrong. Anything that occurred consistently and was accepted by the community was passed on from generation to generation until behaviour patterns were automatically adhered to for the simple reason that 'it was always done that way'; because it was *Maat* (good or right or just). *Maat* was an abstract quality developed by usage and made traditional by strong national observance. The first reference to it is in the Memphite Drama where 'justice was given to him who does what is liked; injustice to him who does what is disliked'. In other words *Maat* at first implied accepted behaviour within the community. The concept developed, with the creation of a God-king, into the spirit of national guidance, for the pharaoh was the head of state and the law. Therefore *Maat* embraced the state machinery and became 'truth' and 'justice'. *Maat* gave stability and authority to the state just as it provided discipline and respect in the family.

The Old Kingdom sages or 'wise men', Imhotep, Kagemni and Ptahhotep, whose instructions and proverbs were quoted for thousands of years after their deaths, provide the earliest formulation to be found in any literature on right conduct. On the question of *Maat*, Ptahhotep wrote: 'Great is "Maat"; its dispensation endures, nor has it been overthrown since the time of its maker, for punishment is inflicted on the transgressor of its laws . . . although misfortune may carry away wealth . . . the power of "Maat" is that it endures, so that a man may say: It is a possession of my father which I have inherited.'

It is from such wholesome wisdoms, addressed from father to son, that we learn most of life in these remote times. It is too common simply to observe the ancient Egyptians' apparent preoccupation with death; it is quite another thing to know of their social experience and learn of their high ethical values, which centred round the family, manners and correct behaviour. To make a long list of the gods and goddesses of ancient Egypt and consequently label the society as 'pagan' is to overlook the heights of their philosophical, social and ethical experience.

The Teachings (Wisdom Literature) in the Old Kingdom were ethical but not religious. Religion (Pyramid Texts) was theological and political, but taught no ethics. What was regarded as correct behaviour was taught by rote within the confines of the family household: Kagemni instructed his children to 'recite it as it is written . . . and it seemed good to them beyond anything in the whole land . . .' The priests, on the other hand, endeavoured to capture a wide audience to promote national unity and economic control under the pharaoh. The ethics of the Instruction literature only appeared in religious texts in the Middle Kingdom (in the form of the 'Negative Confession').

Representations of gods were entirely absent from the private tombs of the Old Kingdom. This is not to say that the ancient Egyptians did not believe that ultimately their conduct on earth would be judged by the 'Great One'. Frequently good deeds were inscribed in tombs. Harkhuf of Elephantine recorded: 'I gave bread to the hungry, clothing to the naked, I ferried him who had no boat . . . I am a worthy and equipped Glorious One . . . As for any man who shall enter into (this) tomb as his mortuary possession, I will seize him like a wild fowl; he shall be judged for it by the Great One.' And the Steward Meni also warned above the doorpost of his tomb: 'Even him who does anything against it [my tomb]. It is the Great God who shall judge [him].' Two things are clear from these texts: first, that the threat of final judgement before the Great God was a deterrent against unacceptable conduct, and secondly, that a man's motive for declaring worthy deeds on earth was 'that it may be well with me in the Great God's presence'. In other cultures in other lands the distinction between good and bad was not to come for the next 2,000 years.

THE PEASANT FARMERS AND WORKMEN

The peasant farmers on the estates lived in houses of sun-dried brick or wattle daubed with clay, not much different from the neolithic houses of their ancestors, with a single room (oblong or square), one door and no windows. Furnishings comprised no more than a rough stool, a box or chest, and perhaps a headrest. Reed mats were hung from the walls, and baskets and earthenware pots were used for storage.

The peasants, who rose with the sun and retired early, wore a loincloth which they frequently cast off during the day. The smaller statues of the Old Kingdom depict an array of good-natured folk: a naked peasant going to market with his sandals in his hand and his shoulder slightly bent beneath the weight of the bag slung over it, for example, or a baker and his wife kneading dough. The tombs of the noblemen, moreover, contain numerous scenes of the poor man's world: fishermen drying fish in the sun or repairing nets and snares, farmers fattening geese or sowing the crops, workers from the vineyard vigorously treading grapes, others in the bakery grinding flour. Both the murals and the inscriptions indicate that the people were happy. The men who carry the nobleman around his estate in a carrying-chair sing that it is as light to bear with their lord seated in it as it is when empty. A musician follows a line of reapers and, as he plays his flute, one of the reapers simultaneously holds a sickle and claps his hands singing the 'Song of the Oxen'. A piper accompanies the harvest. A shepherd leading sheep through the fields sings: 'The shepherd is in the water among the fish; he talks with the *nar*-fish, he passes the time of day with the west-fish . . .' Some of the reliefs are accompanied by texts of conversations between the workers:

> *'That is a very beautiful vessel [you are making].'*
> *'Indeed, it is.'*

> *'I have brought four pots of beer.'*
> *'That's nothing. I loaded my donkeys with 202*
>   *sacks while you were sitting . . .'*

The diet of the people consisted mainly of bread, onions, lentils, vegetables and dried fish. They bartered for their needs. In the tomb representations a loaf of bread is exchanged for some onions, a carpenter's wife gives a fisherman a small wooden

box for some fish, a potter's wife obtains a jar of fragrant ointment for two bowls from her husband's kiln.

The foremen of the various projects appear to have been
more heavily built than their slim and muscular workers. The
famous statue of Ka-aper, known as the 'Sheikh el Balad'
(village chief), shows a heavy, stocky but energetic man striding forward with an acacia staff in his hand. That of Nofir, the
Director of the Granaries, also shows him to be broad in build.
In a mural in the tomb of Ptahhotep is a scene of the foreman,
obese and lazy, seated in a skiff accepting a drink from an
oarsman.

The barracks for the skilled masons at construction sites
were crowded, huddled townships, often a succession of small
chambers beneath a single roof with open passages between.
To the south of Khafre's pyramid are the ruins of a 'pyramid-
town' that must have accommodated the skilled masons
employed on the construction of the tomb. It consisted of long
galleries sub-divided into about ninety-one chambers, each
9½ft wide by 7ft high, and it has been calculated that such
barracks could reasonably have taken 4,000 workers. Presum-
ably the wholesome ideals of Ptahhotep were not widespread
among them.

THE ROYAL FAMILY

The pharaoh of Egypt did not live like a lazy despot. As
vizier he had supervised mining operations, superintended
quarrying operations, controlled the Court of Law and had
been in charge of the Treasury. As pharaoh he was equally
active. He received his advisers and officials, discussed funerary
monuments with his chief architect, and accompanied by his
attendants took inspection tours in his carrying-chair.

Apart from the royal insignia and the richly encrusted
jewelled collars, the royal family dressed little differently from
the landed noblemen. The insignia included the Double
Crown of Upper and Lower Egypt (of which no examples
have been found) and the artificial beard attached to it (many

of these are in the museums of the world). The beard may have been a tradition inherited from their ancestors; being, however, a nation who prided themselves on being clean-shaven, artificial beards were worn as a sign of kingship. The emblems carried by the pharaoh were the crook and flail, both of which had come to indicate regal authority. The tail of a bull and leopard skins were used as insignia by priests and princes.

Naturally the elaborate court etiquette required the pharaoh and his family to have a host of courtiers, retainers and servants. In the royal palace there was a strict and complex structure of rank and classification of work as revealed by the various titles. Each department had its head, who had his own attendants and their appointed helpers There was a Chief Court Physician, a Director of Music, a Chief Manicurist of the Court and even an official who called himself 'He who is Head of the Reversion' and who probably distributed the remains of the five royal meals a day to the people. There was also a Guardian of the Royal Crown and Jewels, a Keeper of the Royal Robes and an Overseer of the Cosmetic Box who 'performed in the matter of cosmetic art to the satisfaction of his lord'. It is from inscriptions of rank and privileges, duties and tasks, that we are informed of life in the royal palace, and the honour that serving the pharaoh was felt to be. Even the 'Sandal-bearer of the King' was proud to record that he did his duties to royal satisfaction, and one retainer boasted in his tomb of the unprecedented privilege of kissing the royal foot rather than the dust before it.

The God-king was no less pious towards his parents or devoted to his children than the noblemen. Many a pharaoh completed the tomb and mortuary temple for his departed father before commencing construction of his own, inscribing his deed on the walls. When Khufu learned that thieves had entered the tomb of his mother Hetep-heres, he ordered a reburial for her in a new, secret tomb at Giza. Unaware that the mummy had already been removed from the sarcophagus, the workers lowered it into a shaft to the east of the Great

Pyramid along with her funerary equipment. It is thanks to Khufu's devotion that the furniture was saved; the only royal furniture to have survived intact from the Old Kingdom. It included the supports and uprights of a royal canopy encased in gold from which mats were hung as curtains to ensure privacy, a royal bed that sloped downwards towards the foot to provide a headrest, two chairs, one of which was portable, and, among the smaller items, an inlaid footboard, vases of gold, copper, and alabaster, gold razors and a gold manicure set. The chairs are magnificently carved with figures of the hawk and the lotus, the symbol of the *Ankh* (Key of Life) and an ibex, all gold-trimmed. The basic design of furniture did not greatly change in later periods.

It is not surprising that Khufu's mother should have had such magnificent funerary equipment. In the 4th dynasty royal blood was carried through the women: as 'Mother of the King of Upper and Lower Egypt' she was herself revered. Just before the fall of the Old Kingdom, in the 6th dynasty, after a process of decentralisation, when pharaohs like Pepi I had married women of non-royal blood, and when noblemen like Ti rose from humble origin to the most powerful positions in the state, legal documents indicate new conditions both on the question of succession and on the position of women. The latter had reduced legal status and, indeed, even after the death of her husband a woman was placed under the guardianship of her eldest son. On his death the responsibility fell on the second, but always the oldest living son was the executor of the deceased's land and entrusted with his funds. He was instructed to guard the property of the family and expressly forbidden to 'share' the wealth entrusted to him.

6

How They Worked

THE working classes can be divided into three categories: the intellectual literates (from whom came physicians, architects and landed noblemen), the craftsmen (including the artists and sculptors) and the peasant farmers and labourers.

MEDICINE

The temples of Heliopolis, Sais and Memphis were centres of learning from earliest times. Here physicians were trained. Such titles as 'Chief of the Dental Physicians' (Hesi-Ra), 'Palace Eye Expert, Physician of the Belly, One Comprehending Internal Fluids and Guardian of the Anus' (Iri), or 'Chief Oculist of the Royal Court' (Wah-Dwa), support Herodotus' observation that there were specialists in ancient Egypt for the different branches of medicine. The Ministry of Health, if one might call it such, comprised the 'Chief of Physicians' and their assistants (non-specialists) under an 'Inspector of Physicians'. Such titles as 'The Chief Physician of Upper Egypt' (Ibi), or 'Greatest Physician of Upper and Lower Egypt' indicate that within the medical profession there was a liaison between distant provinces and the central court.

The medical papyri, of which there are over a score, are clear indication of the advances made in the medical field from very early times. Though the texts date to the Middle and New Kingdoms, it has been established that these were copies (sometimes third and fourth hand) of very early texts. Archaic grammar and obsolete words point to their antiquity as well as certain references to the Old Kingdom. The Berlin medical papyrus, for example, known as the Mother and Child Papyrus, bears a statement that it was found under a statue near Giza in the time of the pharaoh Den (1st dynasty). It further states that after his death it was brought to the pharaoh Sened (2nd dynasty), 'because of its excellence'. The text was signed by 'The Scribe of Sacred Writings, the Chief of the Excellent Physicians, Neterhotep, who prepared the book', (ie he copied it from an original manuscript). The London medical papyrus bears a statement that it was 'brought as a marvel to the Majesty of King Khufu'. And the Edwin Smith surgical papyrus, believed to be the earliest, might have been a copy of the original manuscript of Djer (second pharaoh of the 1st dynasty whose books on anatomy survived, according to Manetho, until Greco/Roman times). It dealt with forty-eight carefully arranged surgical cases of wounds and fractures, detailing a dispassionate examination of the patient and prescribing cures. No ailment was ascribed to the activity of a demonaic power and there was very little magic; the ancient Egyptians were not witch doctors who gave incantations but physicians who prescribed healing remedies and operations. Though some of the cures might be considered rather fanciful—extract of the hair of a black calf to prevent greying—others became famous for their virtue in later times. This was a society where educated men sought methods to prolong life. Beliefs in the potency of spells or exorcisms undoubtedly existed, especially among the lower classes, along with the belief in magical charms and talismans, but magico-religious medicine, as such, only flourished in later times.

Medical and surgical papyri were undoubtedly compiled at different periods, each adding to the limited knowledge of a predecessor. By the 6th dynasty there appears to have been a firmly established medical tradition. For when the vizier Weshptah, architect/friend of the pharaoh Neferirkere, suffered a stroke in the king's presence, he showed great solicitude for his stricken friend and ordered his officials to consult medical documents for a remedy to help the vizier regain consciousness.

Mural reliefs provide further evidence of medical practices. Sesa's tomb at Sakkara (5th dynasty) is known as the Doctor's Tomb in view of the reliefs showing the manipulation of joints. Ankhmahor's tomb (6th dynasty) is known as the Physician's Tomb and shows an operation on a man's toe and the circumcision of a youth—the latter was practised on boys between six and twelve years of age. Finally, we know from mummified bodies that dental surgery was used from early times. Some have teeth extracted, and a 4th-dynasty mummy of a man shows two holes, apparently drilled, beneath a right molar of the lower jaw for draining an abscess. Wooden splints and linen bandages encase broken limbs in pre-dynastic tombs and, indeed, the advances made in mummification indicate a sound knowledge of anatomy.

The highly specialised profession of mummification was not perfected until the New Kingdom. It was performed by priests, as against medicine which was practised by scholars. In the early dynastic period when the bodies of the dead were placed in tombs they were found to perish more quickly than when protected by the warm sand. Since the lifelike appearance was believed essential for a continued existence in the afterlife, artificial means of preservation had to be sought. Early efforts to accomplish this (in the 2nd dynasty) included modelling in clay the features of the face, the genitals and breasts with nipples. This gave an uncannily lifelike appearance. Subsequently, linen strips dipped in resinous material were moulded on to the shrunken body, carefully wrapping individual fingers, etc, the body cavities being filled with linen. Later the intestines and vital organs were removed, wrapped in linen strips and immersed in a natron solution. This development led to the preservation of the viscera in four canopic jars placed in a box (the earliest were those of Khufu's mother).

ARCHITECTURE

Great strides were taken in the field of architecture. The royal tombs of the first two dynasties were large structures with the tomb chamber and surrounding rooms hewn deep in the bedrock surmounted by a superstructure of the characteristic 'palace-façade' panelling. The tombs of the noblemen were strong, low brick structures with rectangular ground-plan and sloping walls for which the word 'mastaba' (bench) was coined by workmen excavating under the French Egyptologist Mariette.

In the 3rd dynasty Zoser's architect, Imhotep, drew up plans for his majestic funerary complex, the central feature of which

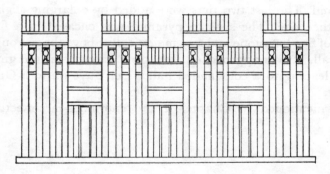

'Palace-façade' panelling of a 1st-dynasty tomb

was the Step Pyramid—the first stone structure in history; Imhotep chose a rectangular site on the Memphite necropolis and marked the corners with stele bearing the names of Zoser and his two daughters. He erected a 30ft high wall round the chosen site using the palace-façade panelling of the earlier dynasties. Imhotep then commenced excavation of the sub-structure and lined the floor of the tomb chamber with granite brought by river from the quarries of Aswan. A series of chambers and a maze of corridors to house the furniture and effects of the deceased were lined with blue tiles.

The superstructure was at first a simple mastaba with a unique square ground-plan. However, a second facing of limestone was then added, 2ft lower than the original wall, thus forming a step. An extension to the east rendered the mastaba rectangular. A series of pits led to a 90ft gallery on the east of the mastaba and it may have been to incorporate these into the tomb that the idea of constructing a second tier first dawned on Imhotep. The ancient Egyptians were still inexperienced in the use of stone, and Imhotep was not an architect with a blueprint so much as an imaginative builder. It was when constructing the third tier that he included in the overall design a mortuary temple and a whole series of dummy buildings. When the fourth tier was raised, the construction could finally be called a Step Pyramid. The last two tiers were added by enlarging slightly on either side. The six-step pyramid was encased in a final layer of fine limestone and rose majestically above the surrounding wall. It was approached through a gateway in the girdle wall, leading to a colonnaded hall which gave on to a Great Court.

As mentioned in Chapter 2 the enormous architectural

Hunting in the marshes (tomb of Mereruka)

significance of Zoser's mortuary complex lies in the fact that Imhotep drew inspiration from the contemporary houses and palaces which have all perished. He transcribed into masonry all light, perishable materials and though his were the first large-scale experiments in stone, he nevertheless provides us with simple elegance and mature expression which is characteristic of the Old Kingdom.

Less than a century lies between the construction of Zoser's Step Pyramid at Sakkara and that of the Great Pyramid of Khufu at Giza. The mastery of stone is reflected, however, in several stages of development. Zoser's successor, Sekhemkhet, also had a Step Pyramid (1). Khaba had what is now known as the Layer Pyramid (2), at Zawiyet el Aryan between Giza and Abu Sir. Nebka's 'Unfinished Pyramid', in the same area, is believed to have been planned on the same lines as Zoser's. A change came with Huni, the last pharaoh of the 3rd dynasty. His pyramid at Meidum (3), though appearing somewhat like a tower today, was the first true pyramid. It was constructed in the form of an eight-step pyramidal monument at a steep angle of $51\frac{1}{4}°$ and, after the steps were filled in, the whole was carefully dressed in stone. The transition having been achieved, Senefru's two pyramids at Dashur, known as the Bent Pyramid

---

Two scenes of musicians, from the tomb of Nenkheftikai

Boatmen's game, from the tomb of Ptahhotep

(4) and the Northern Pyramid (5), show a striving for an architectural ideal that was finally achieved with the perfect symmetry of the three pyramids on the Giza plateau. (See page 107.)

There are no written or pictorial records of the methods used for the planning and construction of the pyramids. Clearly as much engineering know-how as brute force was necessary to raise them. Following such basic considerations as the choice of site—on the western bank of the river, on bedrock free from

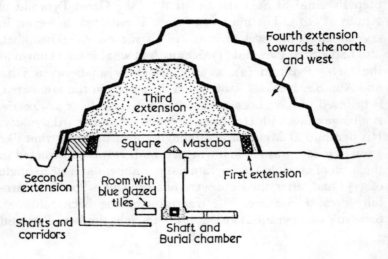

Cross-section of the Step Pyramid. (See p 102)

defects, well above the valley but in close proximity to the river for easy conveyance of stone—was the task of levelling and smoothing the plateau to within a fraction of an inch and orientating the four cardinal points with a maximum error in alignment of little over one-twelfth of a degree.

The building of the great pyramids, has been extensively written about. Some 2,300,000 blocks of sandstone were quarried from Tura on the eastern banks of the Nile, each weighing an average of $8\frac{1}{2}$ tons, they were transported to barges and sailed across the turbulent river in full flood. They

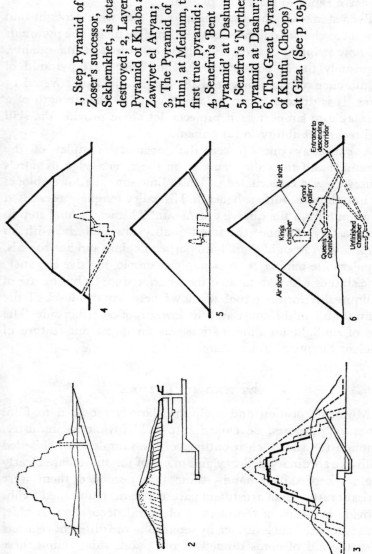

1, Step Pyramid of Zoser's successor, Sekhemkhet, is totally destroyed; 2, Layer Pyramid of Khaba at Zawiyet el Aryan; 3, The Pyramid of Huni, at Meidum, the first true pyramid; 4, Senefru's 'Bent Pyramid' at Dashur; 5, Senefru's 'Northern' pyramid at Dashur; 6, The Great Pyramid of Khufu (Cheops) at Giza. (See p 105)

were then lowered on to rollers and probably manoeuvred up an earth ramp to reach the plateau.

Even stones weighing as much as 16 tons were brought into contact as close as one-five-thousandth of an inch. The pyramids are now stripped of their smooth outer casings of fine-quality, exquisitely fitted, polished limestone. The great pyramid of Khufu once rose to a height of 481 feet and its base covered 13 acres. It is difficult, even today, to visualise the strength of a state able to support such projects, let alone provide the skill and technical ability to raise them.

A causeway once linked the mortuary temples of the pyramids and the valley temples on the river's edge. Khafre's causeway was constructed of white limestone, its lower blocks let into the rock surface beneath. His valley temple was encased in granite from the quarries of Aswan. This was a final step in the mastery of stone: the finest-quality raw material with an emphasis on straight lines, both perpendiculars and horizontals. The 'granite temple' is an example of simple, massive elegance. The statues which decorated the interior were lit by the use of oblique slits forming roof windows between the level of the central aisle of the court and the lower roof on either side. The use of sunlight for illumination was an important feature of ancient Egyptian architecture.

ART AND SCULPTURE

Mural decoration and sculpture, largely required to fulfil funerary purposes, developed into a highly active industry. Though the sharp, clear outlines of the murals were chiselled with extraordinary delicacy and many of the statues are clearly the work of skilled hands, those that fashioned them were artisans rather than artists and part of a team. Unfinished tombs provide evidence of the method of mural decoration. A chief artist prepared each surface by separating the different registers with the aid of cords dipped in red paint, subdividing these further into rows or squares. The sections were then filled with figures of men, animals and hieroglyphic characters, each row representing a single activity. It seems probable that there was a common stock of themes from which a nobleman took his choice, for similar scenes are represented in different tombs with a reduction or increase in the number of individuals, a variation in the placing of inscriptions or the addition of such details as might please the artist: a bald man, a spotted cow, a frisky calf. The arrangement was apparently guided by the artist's preference (within the broad outlines of the customer's wishes) and by the size of the tomb. All available wall space was filled.

A sculptor would carve the figures in low relief, fine detail was added and the finished product was painted. Tomb murals were therefore modelled paintings carried out by a team of artists. Tempera technique was used: natural powdered pigments mixed with water and glue to adhere to the wall surface. Red and yellow were natural desert pigments, chalk or lime provided white and soot black. Copper was the source of the calcined mixture for green, cobalt for blue. The colouring, while not entirely true to nature, was not much exaggerated. For example, clothing was usually white (left without paint on the limestone wall), red ochre was used for the sunburnt bodies of men, while pink, pale brown or yellow was used for women.

In view of the similarity of subject matter, the scenes may appear to be uniform, but close study shows that no two are exactly alike. There was endless modification and, time and again, a human touch. Furthermore, although mural decoration may appear as a mechanical art, the extremely high level of technical and artistic skill, and the harmonious effect should not be overlooked.

The portrait sculptor was the greatest artist of the age. The powerful and lifelike portraits of Khafre and Menkaure, the earliest in the history of art, show fidelity in portraiture and mastery of materials. Khafre had twenty-three cult statues in his valley temple, only five of which have been found; one unique one is carved of diorite.

A statue of Pepi I had an overlay of beaten copper on a carved wooden base and the remarkable painted statues of Rahotep (a prince) and his wife, are amongst the finest examples of Old Kingdom statuary to survive. The sculptors frequently gave a striking effect to the faces, especially those of wood, by inserting pieces of quartz in the eye sockets with a copper stud, which served also as the pupil. All statues show a stress on the faithful reproduction of characteristics. For example, the statue of Khnum-hotep, a dwarf, modelled in refined detail with sturdy legs and corpulent body, is without doubt a masterpiece of realism.

There were certain conventional poses: hands to sides, striding forward or seated, and a strict canon of proportions. Standing figures were 19 units high, and the seated figures were 15 units, the feet were the same length as the height of the head and neck, the distance between the knees and the soles of the feet was twice as long as the feet. Drawing to scale the artist could enlarge a statue, or a scene, accurately. In the tomb of Ti is a representation of an atelier with artisans polishing and carving statues, in accurate likeness of the nobleman. Statues in his tomb show that these were coloured as lifelike as possible. Though these statues were fashioned to house the *Ka* of the deceased, it should be mentioned that statuary was not yet a mechanical art, nor was the portrait sculpture subjected to the mass production of funerary workshops apparent in later periods.

SHIPBUILDING

Egyptians were accomplished sailors, and shipbuilding was one of the most important and oldest industries, the result of the need to travel both within the country, along the Nile, across the Mediterranean and down the Red Sea. The tomb of Ti contains two shipbuilding scenes, Ti presiding over them both, inspecting every stage of the work being carried out. One shows the entire shipbuilding process, from the early stages of shaping and sawing the wooden planks to the last

stages of completion, with workmen milling over the curving
hulls, carving, hammering, sawing and drilling. Seafaring
vessels usually had a curved prow and high stern, each
decorated in the form of a papyrus bud. The centre of the ship
often had an awning. All hinges, nails and bolts were made of
copper, as were the workmen's tools.

One of the oldest texts to survive mentions that during the
reign of Senefru, the 4th-dynasty pharaoh, a fleet of 40 ships
sailed to Lebanon and returned to Egypt laden with timber.
The text mentions that the ships were 100 cubits in length
(178 feet). The nobleman Uni, ordered by royal command to
transport alabaster, constructed a ship '60 cubits in length and
30 cubits in width' and recorded in his tomb that it was
'assembled in seventeen days'. The so-called Solar Boat of
Khufu, discovered in 1954 in a rock-hewn tomb to the south
of the Great Pyramid, is a magnificent barge 143 feet long
constructed of cedar from Lebanon. It had been completely
dismantled to fit into the tomb, but careful reassembly dis-
closed a flat-bottomed boat with a massive curving hull rising to
elegant prow and stern posts. Poles on the deck proved to be the
supporting palm-shaped columns of a large roofed cabin.
Steering oars, each 16½ feet long, were also found, and coils of
rope. This was the first royal barge discovered—other boat
pits dating to the early dynasties were empty. Examination of
the vessel indicates that it actually sailed and the planks
were 'sewn' together by a system of ropes through holes that
met in pairs on the inside. The term 'Solar Boat', coined when
it was first discovered in the belief that it was for funerary
purposes (to take the departed pharaoh across the sky to join
the heavenly gods), is somewhat misleading. Such ships
probably served the pharaoh in his capacity as King of Upper
and Lower Egypt during his lifetime, and were buried with
him as part of his funerary equipment after his death. Another
pit is known to exist to the south of the Great Pyramid: not
yet excavated, it is believed to contain a second vessel.

LESSER INDUSTRIES

Other industries produced leather, papyrus, bricks, glass, pottery, jewellery and copperware. The coppersmith, who supplied the tools necessary for shipbuilding, quarrying stone for funerary monuments and for fashioning murals and statues, had a busy workshop. It was also his responsibility to make copper drains for the earliest plumbing and the various implements required for agriculture. Craftsmen of high order developed from early times and there was a tendency for children to ply the trades of their fathers, at first making themselves useful around the workshops and then working as apprentices.

The tomb of Ti records the goldsmith's factory and the different stages of the production of jewellery. Ti himself watches the head goldsmith weighing the precious metal that was brought from the alluvial sands of the eastern desert, while scribes record it. Workers are depicted casting, soldering and fitting together a rich assortment of fine jewellery. Six men direct their blowpipes to the flames in a clay furnace. Beside them a workman pours the molten metal. On the extreme right four men beat gold-leaf. Some of the engravers who are seated on low benches are dwarfs. Pieces of turquoise, cut or ground into tiny pieces, are inlaid with precision, soldered and fitted into exquisite necklets and other items of adornment.

Carpentry was a highly developed industry. As already mentioned furniture was often overlaid with gold and silver. Carpenters used hammers and mallets, saws with teeth slanting towards the handle indicating that they were pulled not pushed, and bow-drills for making holes. Leather-production, too, had long been mastered and the curing of hides produced soft, fine-quality skins. These were dyed in various colours and used to cover stools, chairs, beds and cushions as well as to fashion sandals.

The glass-maker supervised the production of multi-coloured

glass bottles and vases which were widely exported. Tiles were also decorated by spreading the molten liquid and glazing them with rich colour. These were used to adorn palace and tomb walls. Although serving a utilitarian purpose, most of the products manufactured in ancient Egypt were fashioned with a fine sense of balance and an unconscious desire for beauty. Stone vessels, for example, were created in perfect symmetry, the flint borers with which they were made in pre-dynastic times were superseded by a cranked brace with weights acting as a flywheel for hollowing. Unfortunately the ancient industry of stone-vessel manufacture was largely outmoded by the potter when he began to fashion his ware with the aid of a horizontal wheel. Deftly guiding the swirling vessel with his hands, his rate of production was much larger, and he was able to fulfil the demand for vessels for storage and eating purposes. Egypt was rich in clays, and pottery was produced on a large scale. By the Old Kingdom, the days of irregular burning in an open fire at the mercy of the wind had passed; the potter had rows of closed furnaces to achieve uniform firing.

AGRICULTURE

The bulk of the population, however, was employed on the land or in agriculture-related industries like viticulture, papyrus-manufacture, spinning and weaving. The agricultural cycle comprised three seasons. The *Akhet*, the season of the inundation, which began on 19 July, the *Perit* ('going out'), the season for ploughing and sowing which began on 15 November, and *Shemu*, the harvest, which began on 16 March.

With the rise of the Nile the peasants made sure that their cattle were safely housed on dry land and, with agricultural activities suspended, cared for them and provided them with food already laid in storage. They carefully directed the water from the main canals to smaller branches transversing the fields in straight or curved lines, and controlled it by means of embankments. When the water level began to fall these natural reservoirs retained a residue of mineral-rich sediment which was ready to receive seed without further preparation. Thrown on the surface the seed was usually trodden by goats. Where, however, the earth dried hard, a plough was used. The hoe, one of the most ancient of agricultural tools consisted of a broad, pointed blade of wood attached to a handle at an acute angle and held in position in the centre by a slack rope. The plough was a hoe enlarged by adding two long wooden arms on which the ploughman could lean to keep the furrow straight and also to pressure the blade into the soil. A pole was provided with a yoke for attaching to draught animals.

Although the Nile valley and the Delta were fertile, full exploitation of the land only came with unremitting toil. Naturally the peasants, from centuries of experience, had gradually become aware of the potential. They had determined the most suitable times for sowing and reaping, and the most rewarding systems of irrigation for the different areas. In the temple of the 5th-dynasty pharaoh Nyuserre the life of the peasant is depicted during the seasonal operations throughout the course of a single year. From these and from scenes in the tombs of noblemen it is clear that the harvest was the season of most strenuous activity. The ripened corn was reaped with the aid of a sickle, placed in sacks and loaded on to donkeys to be carried to the threshing floor. The ears of corn were then taken from the sacks and piled in heaps to be trodden by oxen, goats or donkeys. The threshed grain was piled in a heap by means of three-pronged forks and sifted and winnowed by two small boards or scoops. The latter were used in pairs for tossing the unhusked grain into the wind. Finally the grain was placed in sacks by women and transported to the granary.

Flour was ground by placing grain at the upper end of a slightly hollowed, slanting slab of limestone and sliding a crossbar of sandstone across it. The ground flour gradually worked downwards and was caught in a tray at the lower end.

Flax was also cultivated in large quantities. It was harvested at different times for different purposes: when ripe, the fibres tough, it was suitable for mats and ropes. If cut when the stems were green, it could be woven into fine soft cloth: some of the surviving remnants show that the fabric was sometimes of such gossamer fineness as to be almost indistinguishable from silk. This was particularly the case with royal linen, though coarser textiles were woven on a more widespread scale. Weaving was carried out by women, who also made tapestries. The latter were either for hanging on the walls of noblemen's villas, or to form the shade of a roof garden.

Viticulture was one of the most highly developed, as well as one of the earliest, industries. The first wine-press hieroglyphic dates from the 1st dynasty, and there is evidence that even from this early date wine was transported across the country in sealed jars. Grapes were plucked by hand, placed in vats and trodden until the liquid ran through holes into a waiting container. Fermentation probably occurred naturally, due both to the method of pressing and the high summer temperature. Date-palm wine was also produced.

The manufacture of papyrus paper was another flourishing industry. The papyrus, sliced into thin sections, was laid side by side and crosswise, soaked and compressed. Beating and drying turned it into sheets of durable paper. Two rolls of papyrus in a box dating to the reign of the 1st-dynasty pharaoh Udimu are evidence of how early it was produced. Ships trading with the Phoenician coast carried bales of this essentially Egyptian product as cargo. The papyrus plant served many purposes: the stalks were woven and used as mats, the vegetable fibres were transformed into a pliable, tough material suitable for sandals, and lightweight skiffs for hunting in the marshes were made by binding long bundles together.

Veterinary medicine was practised by the peasants and the obvious health of the herds indicates proficient rearing. It was a talent handed from father to son. In the tomb of Ptahhotep a scene shows a cow giving birth with the aid of a veterinary surgeon who gently guides the calf into the world. The ancient Egyptians knew their animals intimately, took great care of them and often fed them by hand. In the tomb of Ti a cow is being milked by a cowherd while the overseer leans on his staff watching. Though there are scenes of herdsmen driving rams across a canal with raised whip, none shows an animal being beaten.

CHANCES OF PROMOTION

The working classes had every hope of rising above that station into which they were born, either by marriage, inheritance or promotion. Evidence is available from the autobiographical accounts in the tombs of the noblemen. Since provisions for the afterlife had to be commensurate with a man's social standing, lists of offerings in the tombs grew larger and larger as the power and wealth of a man increased. It finally occurred to the tomb owners that a simple offering prayer would be adequate substitute for a long offering list. A similar short-cut was sought for the inscriptions identifying the titles and ranks of the owners of the tombs: as these grew longer they gradually developed into autobiographical renditions. Metjen's is one of the oldest. He died in the reign of Senefru and was buried near Zoser's temple on the Sakkara necropolis (his tomb has been transported to Berlin and reconstructed in the Museum). The text tells of his gradual rise from Scribe and Overseer of the Stores to Governor of a number of towns and districts in the eastern Delta. For his administrative prowess he was rewarded with gifts of land on which he built a house '200 cubits long, 200 cubits wide' and surrounded by a walled garden.

One of the best-known cases of a rise in rank in the Old Kingdom was that of Uni (already met in Chapter 4). A man of humble birth, he started his career as a minor official under the pharaoh Teti, and rose to the position of 'Favoured Courtier' under Pepi. In ancient Egypt a man who proved fit in performing one task (albeit solving a case of treason in the royal harem) was considered equally fit for others. Entrusted with supervising a group of workmen bringing a block of stone suitable for the pharaoh's sarcophagus, Uni performed the task so efficiently—transporting it complete with lid, doorway, lintel and two jambs for the tomb as well as a libation table—that, as seen, the pharaoh forthwith put him in charge of a body of troops detailed for an expedition against hostile tribes in the eastern desert, and the nomadic tribes of Nubia. Uni's success on five different occasions was rewarded by a requisition from the treasury to procure labour for the quarrying and transportation of a sumptuous sarcophagus for his own tomb. Uni was by this time one of the highest dignitaries of the court, being awarded the distinction of being permitted to bear a staff and wear sandals in the presence of the pharaoh. 'Never,' he inscribed in his tomb, 'has the like been done for any servant.' 'I was excellent in the heart of His Majesty beyond any official of his, beyond any noble of his, beyond any servant of his . . .'

Many persons of obscure origin or even base servitude rose to high honours and died governors of provinces or ministers of the pharaoh. Ti, the vigorous nobleman of the 5th dynasty who served under three pharaohs, was not of royal blood, yet his marriage to the princess Nefer-Hotep-s gave him a special position and his children ranked with royalty. There is considerable evidence of the close relationship between a pharaoh and his officials. Frequently a pharaoh confided in his most favoured official who bore the title 'Friend' and who claimed to be 'uniquely loved'. A reward even greater than promotion was a pharaoh's contribution to the building of a nobleman's tomb. Debhen inscribed that his lord was 'so satisfied with him' that he detailed some two score men and ten to complete his tomb for him, quarry two false doors of stone and supply blocks for the façade as well as the statue to house his *Ka*. Weshptah, the architect/vizier who suffered a stroke and died despite medical attention, was furnished with a tomb and magnificent ebony coffin. Sebni, it will be remembered, was the loyal son who set out on a rescue mission to recover his father's body from the south and bring it back to Egypt for burial. On his return journey he sent his officer Iri and two companions ahead to the court with products from the south and instructions to bring back the necessary equipment for embalming the body. Sebni's mission was so highly regarded by the pharaoh that he sent a military escort to meet him, and rewarded him by assisting in the embalming and burial of his father, and presenting him with a gift of land for himself.

At all levels of the bureaucratic system there was, of course, a tendency to inherit posts, as, for example among the scribes. In the cemetery at Giza, is a whole dynasty of small-scale scribes (the distinction being drawn between the literates who registered cattle, held the post of clerk in the Double Granary, etc. and the scribes who were scholars, sages, physicians and philosophers). Whatever his social standing, a scribe had a most respected profession and was in a position to attract the notice of his superiors.

The relationship between the noblemen and their foremen and workers is clear from such inscriptions as: 'whether craftsmen or quarrymen, I satisfied them'. One 4th-dynasty nobleman was more explicit: in an inscription on the base of his statue he declared that the sculptor that fashioned his statue 'was satisfied with the reward I gave him'.

Sentiments common among the inscriptions of the tombs at Sakkara were: 'Never did I use force against any man, for I wanted my name to be good before God and my repute to be good before all men.' And 'Never did I do an evil thing.'

Such inscriptions may have been the result of a man wishing to stress his qualities for his name to shine before the 'Great God'. However, they encourage us to view, at least with some reservation Herodotus' description of hordes of oppressed and overworked slaves, whipped by merciless overseers, toiling and dying in the scorching sun in order to raise a monumental pyramid to the glorification of their God-king. There were in fact few slaves in the Old Kingdom, since foreign conquest was at a minimum; there were no worker revolts until later periods; and the marks made on some of the casing stones delivered from the quarries indicate a spirit of pride and competition among the workers (largely recruited from the peasant community during high Nile) who called themselves 'Vigorous Gang', 'Enduring Gang', etc.

Ptahhotep, the 5th-dynasty sage who instructed his son to prepare him for the official duties that lay ahead of him, gave much advice on behaviour that would ensure success in official circles, and the attitudes to be taken towards both betters and subordinates. 'If he above you is one who was formerly of very humble station, have no knowledge of his former low estate . . . be respectful towards him because of what he has achieved; for substance cometh not of itself.' Or conversely: 'If thou has become great after thou wert little, and hast gained possessions after thou wert formerly in want . . . be not unmindful of how it was with thee before. Be not boastful of thy wealth, which has come to thee as a gift of the god. Thou art not greater than another like thee to whom the same has happened.'

Ptahhotep had some shrewd advice on the matter of being helpful to one's employer, for: 'thy food hangs upon his mood, the belly of one loved is filled, thy back shall be clothed thereby . . .'

Table manners, especially at an official dinner given by one of higher station, were considered important: 'Take when he gives to thee what he puts before thee, but do not look at what is before *him*, look at what is before *thee*, and shoot him not with many glances . . . Turn thy face downward until he addresses thou and speak only when he addresses thee. Laugh when he laughs, so shalt thou be very agreeable to his heart and what thou doest will be very pleasant to his heart . . .'

Whereas Ptahhotep had much to say on behaviour in the presence of superiors: 'If you meet one superior to you, fold your arms, bend your back. To flout him will not make him agree with you . . . ', he particularly stresses: 'If you meet a poor man, not your equal, do not attack him because he is weak . . . wretched is he who injures a poor man . . .'

A nobleman's attitude towards his subordinates is

particularly apparent through Ptahhotep's enumeration of the qualities of leadership: 'If thou art a man who leads, seek out every beneficent deed, that thy conduct may be blameless . . .' 'If thou art an administrator, be gracious when thou hearest the speech of a petitioner.'

A man is recognised by that which he knows.
His heart is the balance for his tongue;
His lips are correct when he speaks,
and his eyes in seeing;
his ears together hear what is profitable for his son,
who does righteousness and is free from lying.

Established is the man whose standard is righteousness,
who walketh according to its way.

7

How They Spent Their Leisure Time

Leisure was made possible by the economy, exceptional opportunities and favourable climate. Almost all the tombs of the noblemen at Sakkara and Giza contain scenes of the deceased with his family seated beneath an arbour enjoying the mild north breeze, or with friends or relatives being entertained by musicians, dancers and singers. Moreover the panorama of everyday life indicates how vitally conscious the people were of the animal and bird life teeming around them and how much they esteemed the great outdoors. It seems that among the greatest pleasures were venturing into the marshes in search of aquatic birds, hunting in the undulating plains of the desert and fishing in canals and lakes.

The ancient Egyptians had a great sense of rhythm and love of music. During important national events (for example, the breaking of ground by the 'Scorpion King' depicted on his historically important mace-head), a line of women clapped in unison. A piper or singer often entertained fishermen and farmers while they worked. Not surprisingly, we find the wealthy classes enjoying music at all times of day, at their morning toilet, at meals and during leisure hours. Harps were small and usually played by a seated musician. Flutes were in two sizes and a full orchestra comprised two harps and two flutes. Two or three musicians as well as singers and clappers usually accompanied lithe young maidens as they performed dances for the pleasure of the nobleman and his family. One such scene, in the tomb of Ti, shows both male and female performers. The dancers raise their arms in a circular motion above their heads while their feet move forward; a gesture probably repeated to the rhythm of the music. A more energetic performance is depicted in the tomb of Ankhmahor where the dancers do a high kick, and in the tomb of Kagemni an acrobatic dance is performed by young girls who are depicted with the left foot placed flat on the floor, torso curved, head dropping backwards until the hair, plaited into a pigtail with decoration on the end, hangs down in perfect symmetry.

Entertainment brings to mind the story of the pigmy brought from the Land of Yam to amuse the young pharaoh Pepi II. It is one of the most appealing tales of the Old Kingdom. Pepi was only six years old when he ascended the throne. During the second year of his reign, Harkhuf, a nobleman of Elephantine, returned from the south with exotic products and a dancing pigmy as a gift for the king. He sent messengers ahead to inform the pharaoh of what to expect and with great enthusiasm Pepi sent a letter of thanks to Harkhuf requesting him to take every precaution that the pigmy should arrive in Memphis in good condition. Harkhuf was instructed to put trustworthy persons in charge on the boat so as to ensure the pigmy should not fall overboard, and that when he slept guards should sleep on either side of the cabin and make an inspection ten times a night. 'For', wrote Harkhuf in his tomb where he recorded the entire episode and quoted the letter in his biographical text, 'My Majesty desires to see this pigmy more than all the gifts of Setjru, Irtjet and Yam.'

A legend in the Westcar Papyrus tells of the aged king Senefru being otherwise entertained. A magician recommended that he row on the palace lake in the company of 'all the beauties who are in your palace chamber . . . The heart of Your Majesty shall be refreshed at the sight of their rowing as they row up and down. You can see the beautiful fish ponds of your lake, and you can see the beautiful fields around it [and] your heart will be refreshed at this.' Senefru forthwith ordered that twenty oars be made of ebony, fitted with gold and silver, and instructed that twenty women be brought, 'the most beautiful in form, with hair well braided, with firm breasts, not yet having opened up to give birth. Let there be brought to me twenty nets, and let these nets be given to these women when they have taken off their clothes. Then it was done according to all that His Majesty commanded, and they rowed up and down. The heart of His Majesty was happy at the sight of their rowing.'

OUTDOOR SPORT

Hunting was popular among all classes. The pharaoh Sahure is depicted hunting gazelle, antelope, deer and other animals. Most of the noblemen may be seen pursuing wild game and capturing different species. And the working classes chased gazelle, oryx, wild oxen, hares and ostrich with equal enthusiasm. Long bow and arrow, lasso, throwing sticks and *bola* were the most common hunting weapons. The bow was no more than 3 feet in length and the arrows, carried in leather quivers, came in several varieties; the one preferred for hunting (which survived into the New Kingdom) had an agate arrowhead cemented to a sturdy, usually ebony, stick which was fitted into a hollow reed shaft. The latter was decorated with two feathers and notched for the bowstring.

Considerable ability must have been required in the handling of the throwing stick, numerous specimens of which may be found in most of the museums of the world. They, too, varied in shape, some being semi-circular and others ending in a knob. The *bola* consisted of a rope or strap about 16 feet long with a single rounded stone attached to the end. When thrown, the cord would twist round the legs or neck of the animal and hinder its movement; a good hunter could bring down an animal by his strength. The lasso differed from the *bola* in having no stone attached: the noose would merely be thrown round the neck of the running victim—gazelle, wild goat, water-buck, and ostrich.

Hunting scenes were extremely spirited, showing the hunter enthusiastically pursuing game in an obvious display of pleasure. Some scenes indicate how bait was used. In Ptahhotep's tomb the muzzle of a young tethered heifer is being seized in the jaws of a lion, which a hunter points out to his two hounds before setting them loose. Hounds were specially trained for hunting and following wounded beasts. Every effort seems to have been made to save them from being hurt and to capture game alive. Ptahhotep is depicted watching men dragging cages containing lion, a frame with gazelles bound together in groups, and smaller cages containing hedgehogs. Sometimes a hunter, perhaps after killing its mother, would take a young gazelle back to the village.

The Egyptians were avid fishermen. After the waters of the annual flood receded, ponds were left in the open country. These, as well as the canals and the river, yielded an inexhaustible supply of mullet, catfish, telapia, perch, barbel and other varieties of fish. The upper classes penetrated deeply into the thickets in their firmly constructed papyrus skiffs, their feet squarely placed on the central plank. They pursued fish with spears—sometimes two-pronged—but never angled. The crew, on the other hand, sometimes speared fish like their masters but more often angled from small boats, using as many as five hooks on a single line. Drag-nets were drawn from the shore in small canals, trawl-nets were used in larger canals and rivers, and trap-nets were also used. These were wicker-like baskets with narrow necks, sometimes curving inwards; when dropped in shallow water, the fish would be attracted to the bait and swim inside but could not emerge. Hippo-hunting with spears was popular among all classes.

The familiarity of the ancient Egyptians with bird life is particularly apparent from the tomb of Ti, where various species of the marshes are depicted in families near their nests, each drawn with characteristic features and easily identifiable (although not drawn to scale). They include quail, partridge, heron, pelican, turtledove, magpie, swallow, wild duck and goose, among others, and wading in the reedy swamps near the river are flamingoes, pelicans and cormorants. In fact indigenous and migratory waterfowl were so plentiful that the ancient Egyptians likened a crowd to a bird pond during the inundation. Birds were most often caught in clap-nets. Hunting them with a throw-stick was also an extremely popular sport which needed skill; the hunter, often accompanied by his wife, children and servants, had to stand firmly in his boat with legs wide apart and, whilst maintaining his balance, fling the missile at the fowl as they took to the air. Some of the men with him hold decoy-birds, indicating that the boat made its way quietly through the thickets to creep up on the fowl. Mongooses were trained to catch small aquatic birds, considered a great delicacy.

It is not surprising, in view of the warm weather and the proximity of the river, that the ancient Egyptians were swimmers from early times. A hieroglyph of the name of a man, depicted on an Old Kingdom offering-table, shows a man swimming, and it is evident from this and other representations that the crawl stroke was common to them. Learning to swim may, indeed, have been necessary training for children among the upper classes, for a biographical inscription of a Middle Kingdom nobleman referred to the encouragement his pharaoh gave him and declared that as a youth 'he caused me to take swimming lessons along with the royal children'.

In many tombs the owner is depicted watching boatmen's games which may have been either an exhibition contest or a race. Light reed boats, often filled with produce, were punted in the same direction. Meanwhile two or three men stood in each boat equipped with long poles with which they tried to push their opponents into the water. They would then either board the 'enemy' boat or tip it over.

In the tombs of the Old Kingdom only children (identified by the side-lock of youth) are depicted playing games, whilst in the Middle Kingdom young men and women are also shown in sports activities. Moreover, in the Old Kingdom most of the games are played by boys and, with few exceptions, boys and girls did not play together. A game requiring skill was played by boys with sharp pointed sticks which they raised and threw at a target on the ground between them. A 'tug-of-war' trial of strength was accompanied by such inscriptions as 'Your arm is much stronger than his', 'My team is stronger than yours' and 'Hold fast comrades.' Boys played a high-jump game, leaping over an obstacle formed by two of their comrades sitting opposite each other with soles of the feet and tips of the fingers touching. In another game a boy kneels on the ground with one leg outstretched; his comrades endeavour to touch him lightly with their feet while avoiding his hands. Whoever he catches takes his place on the ground.

A girls' game is depicted in Mereruka's tomb: two players in the centre hold either two or four partners with outstretched arms; the latter lean outwards so that only their heels touch the ground. The text reads: 'Turn around four times.' Though there are no murals of children playing ball in the Old Kingdom, balls have been found, even in prehistoric graves. Some were covered in leather, cut into sections, sewn together and filled with fine straw or reeds. Others were made of wood or clay, in one or more colours.

INDOOR GAMES

The ancient Egyptians were also imaginative in their indoor recreation. A favourite game appears to have been similar to draughts, played on a rectangular board divided into thirty or thirty-three squares. Carved black and white pawns were used. Though the players have been depicted facing each other, there is no indication of the rules of the game. The earliest gaming piece (in the shape of a house with sloping roof) was found in the tomb of the 1st-dynasty pharaoh Udimu (Den). Pre-dynastic 'pieces' of clay coated with wax were, however, found with a checker-board table of unbaked clay held up by four thick short legs and divided into eighteen squares on the surface.

A game which appears to have been popular in the Old Kingdom was played with a series of discs about 4 inches in diameter, made in wood, horn, ivory, stone and copper, each with a hole in the centre through which a 6-inch pointed stick was inserted. These were usually found alongside wooden trays which unfortunately all perished, leaving us with no indication of how the game was played. Perhaps the stick was rotated between the palms of the hands to make the discs spin like a top.

Some of the Old Kingdom games did survive its fall. One such was played on a low table, its surface displaying an engraved or inlaid coiled snake, the head situated at the centre of the board and the body divided into transverse lines forming segments. The 'pieces' for this game comprised three lions, three lionesses and five red-and-white balls; these were kept in an ebony box when the game was over. Many 1st-and 2nd-dynasty tombs have yielded these.

STORIES AND FESTIVALS

Story-telling played an important part in the lives of the ancient Egyptians. Their oral tradition must be set apart from the Teachings or 'Wisdom' literature (Chapter 6) and the religious texts (Chapter 3). The deeds of gods and kings were not written in early times and only found their way through verbal tradition into the literature of a later date. This treasury of popular tale was based on an ageless tradition in ancient Egypt. As we have seen the people, their society and their institutions were moulded by the environment and by nature's changeless cycles. This stability of the physical environment resulted in the lives of the rural Egyptians remaining changeless. For, while the priestly politicians were striving for political control and the sages were teaching proverbs and behaviour to their sons, the life of the peasants was moulded, as in times long past, by the rise and fall of the Nile. Each evening when the sun set, his work was done. He would put aside his hoe, his sickle and his winnowing fork, and sit with his friends in the villages of sun-dried brick, or on the rocky outcrop overlooking the valley, and tell tales.

They related all they knew of their ancient kings, especially of the first pharaoh who united the Two Lands and who, like themselves, knew how to exploit the waters of the Nile. Narmer, they told, diverted the great river through an artificial channel and constructed a moat round his city which was fed by the river. They told tales of the good and kindly king Senefru who helped the poor; of the wicked Khufu who constructed a mighty tomb in the shape of the sacred *ben-ben* at Heliopolis, and of Menkaure who was good and just and compensated the poor. Popular and magical tales were closely bound together in a 'Thousand and One Nights' narrative which provided a reason for their telling, like the magical feats performed in the various reigns of the Old Kingdom (Westcar Papyrus—Chapter 3). When the farmers told their sons certain stories of the battles between Horus and Set, they were telling them their ancient history of battles between Upper and Lower Egypt (during the first two dynasties). And in telling them others they were explaining the triumph of the fertile valley over the arid desert. If some of the tales had long been woven to serve a politico-religious purpose and subtly guide their loyalties, the farmers were unaware of it.

They told tales of the world around them: how the sky was held aloft by mountain peaks or pillars that rose above the range that formed the edge of the world; how the sun was a disc of fire that sailed across the heavens in a boat; how the sky was a mother-goddess, Nut, who supported the heavenly bodies and the earth was the God Geb who sprouted vegetation. They told that through the centre of the land flowed the river which rose from the eternal ocean in the south and joined the eternal ocean in the north.

They told tales of their river: how Hapi the Nile-god dwelt in a grotto on an island where the Nile rose from the eternal ocean in the south and from whence he controlled its flow to the ocean in the north; of the terrible famine in the reign of their ancient king Djet when the river failed to rise because the people had not made sufficient sacrifices to Hapi.

And they told tales of their land: how the vegetation which died with the harvest was reborn when the grain sprouted, just as the Sun-god 'died' each evening and was reborn the next morning. How the Desert-god, Set, the personification of drought, darkness and evil, secretly aspired to the throne of Osiris, the god of fertility and water. They told how, when Horus was but a child and had been hidden in the marshes of the Delta, he was bitten by Set who had taken the form of a poisonous snake. Isis, in despair, called to the heavens for help, and the 'Boat of Millions of Years', drawing the Sun-god and his retinue across the heavens, heard her. Ra the Sun-god sent Thoth to speak to Isis and offer help. Thoth informed her that the boat of the Sun-god would stand still, darkness would reign, there would be no food and the people of the earth would suffer until Horus was cured. They told how the evil of Set was overcome, Horus became healthy and the Sun-god resumed his journey across the heavens, cast his rays upon the earth and caused the crops to grow again.

Rural festivals were a great source of pleasure. They were closely allied with the working patterns of the people, and were based on the agricultural cycle. The Nile festivals heralding the arrival of the flood were at once the most solemn and most joyous in the land. Sacrifices would be made to ensure that the waters rose to the required height to assure a bounteous return from the land, and prayers of thanks would be offered. The celebrations heralding the rebirth of the crop, the reaping of the first sheaf, the opening of a new canal, the bearing of the crop to the granary, were all accompanied by hand-clapping and singing. Some festivals were celebrated simultaneously throughout the land, others were local, all were of a religious

129

nature. Pilgrimages might be made to the shrines of local deities to present offerings, or a longer journey might be undertaken to the shrine of a more widely popular deity to make a sacrifice. These were not gestures of piety towards the gods (a sentiment common in the New Kingdom), but a self-imposed duty, a gratification and a familiar and recognised pattern of behaviour.

In the Old Kingdom the people were confident (they knew not war or foreign occupation), hard-working (a reflection of a stable and organised government), and optimistic (since the nature worship of Osiris had not yet developed into a Cult of the Dead there was no need for them to defend themselves against the awesome powers of the underworld and they suffered no apprehension of the hereafter). When they died and were buried on the western bank of the Nile, along with the necessary provisions for the hereafter, they would go to the 'Godly West' and live again, exactly as on earth. The eternity envisaged by the people was understandably a peasant environment as befitted a peasant community. There would be no hunger or want. They would till the fields, breathe the fresh air along the river banks, fish in the bulrushes, paddle boats along the river and enjoy fowling and hunting for ever and ever in the 'Field of Reeds'.

8

What Survives from the Ancient Egyptian World

NOWHERE on earth are there more plentifully preserved monuments and relics of an ancient civilisation than in Egypt. They have sustained the ravages of time, vandalism, invasions, conquests and grave-robbers. The tombs and temples were built on such a grand scale, the murals and statues executed with such artistic skill, and craftsmanship had reached such a degree of perfection, that they will ever lure man to a realisation of his heritage. 'Egypt contains more wonders than any other land, and is pre-eminent above all the countries in the world for works that one can hardly describe,' wrote Herodotus.

Though much of Egypt's portable treasure today adorns the museums of the world, the Egyptian Museum in Cairo naturally boasts the most valuable and comprehensive collection. Founded by the French Egyptologist Mariette in 1881, its contents are arranged in chronological order (though the heavier stone statues, stele and sarcophagi are on the ground floor). They range from neolithic artifacts and pottery to statues and portraits of the Greco-Roman period; five thousand years of Egypt's ancient history. There are statues, stele, murals, sarcophagi, texts, jewellery, etc, of all periods, including the Hetep-Heres collection of royal furniture of the Old Kingdom, the famous Tutankhamon Collection, a Collection of the Tanite Kings (21st/22nd dynasty) which represents the largest collection of gold and silver work in the museum, the Ikhnaton Collection including statues of the pharaoh himself, exquisite paintings from his Sun Temple at Tel el Amarna, and a superb bust (unpainted) of his wife Neferteti. There is also a Mummy Room containing forty mummies of some of Egypt's most important pharaohs (including Amenhotep I, Thutmose II and III, Seti I, and Ramses II and III) which were recovered from a shaft at Der el Bahri (Luxor), where they had been hidden by the priests of the 21st dynasty for safety against grave robbers.

Most of the works described in this study may be found in the Egyptian Museum, including the famous diorite statue of Khafre, statues of Menkaure between Hathor and local deities, the 'Sheikh el Balad', Ra-Hotep and Nofret, the copper statue of Pepi I and his son, the statue of Ti, the nobleman whose tomb we have described in detail, and the granite sarcophagus of Menerre (procured by Uni who excavated five canals at the First Cataract to transport the barges to Memphis) to mention but a few. These, of course, are apart from objects of a non-funerary nature: combs, mirrors, furniture, weapons, tools, etc.

The contents of the Museum, however, represent but a small part of Egypt's treasures, for indeed the whole of the Nile Valley is an outdoor museum. Following the ancient highway, the river Nile, we will briefly view some of the surviving monuments that lie between Giza, opposite Cairo, where the Great Pyramids straddle the desert plateau, and Abu Simbel, over 600 miles further south, where the gigantic statues of Ramses II sit in massive dignity at the entrance of his famous temple above the waters of Lake Nasser.

Giza

On the western bank of the Nile, about 6 miles south-west of Cairo are the greatest monuments of the Old Kingdom: the Pyramids of Giza. That of Khufu has the distinction of being the largest single building ever constructed. The Solar Boat (Chapter 6) has been reassembled in a special museum on the southern flank of the pyramid (not yet open to the public). The pyramid of Khafre, the second pyramid, is the most complete example of a royal tomb complex in the Old Kingdom. It comprises the pyramid itself, its mortuary temple and a causeway of white limestone connecting it to a valley temple, sometimes known as the Granite Temple. Nearby is the Sphinx, the huge figure of a recumbent lion with human head which is believed to have been carved in the features of the pharaoh Khafre. Its total length is 240 feet and between its paws is a huge red granite stele narrating the dream of the pharaoh Thutmose IV (18th dynasty) who, whilst resting in the shadow of the Sphinx after a hunting expedition, heard the voice of his 'father' the Sun-god, ordering him to deliver him from the suffocating desert sands. The Sun-god demanding release from the sand was the Sphinx itself which, by the New Kingdom, was understood to be a combination of the Sun-gods Ra-Atum-Keper-Harakhte.

To the south of Menkaure's pyramid are the ruins of the village that accommodated the skilled masons who were employed on the construction of the pyramid (Chapter 5) and where all the needs of the workmen were prepared.

Abu Sir

The pyramids of Abu Sir are almost completely in ruin. However, the splendid reliefs which adorn the funerary temple of the 5th-dynasty pharaoh Sahure include the first surviving representation of seagoing ships. There are also fine sculptured reliefs of various aspects of rural life throughout the agricultural year as well as hunting scenes depicting the pharaoh accompanied by dogs pursuing antelope, gazelle, deer and other small animals.

Sakkara

This is one of the richest archaeological sites in Egypt. It preserves relics from all periods of ancient Egyptian history. Those described in this book include the royal tombs of the 1st dynasty (Chapter 2), Zoser's Step Pyramid Complex (Chapters 2 and 6), 5th- and 6th-dynasty tombs of noblemen decorated in painted relief (Chapters 5, 6 and 7), and the pyramids of the 6th-dynasty pharaohs which contain columns of inscribed hieroglyphics painted in blue and known as the Pyramid Texts (Chapter 3).

Another highlight at Sakkara is the Serapeum, or Apis Tombs. These are a series of subterranean galleries, hewn out of solid rock containing the remains of bulls. Though the Apis bull was regarded as sacred in Memphis from early times, the Serapeum has not been discussed in this study since the Apis cult only developed in exaggerated form in the New Kingdom. The first common grave dates to the reign of the 19th-dynasty pharaoh Ramses II, a new gallery was excavated in the reign of the 26th-dynasty pharaoh Psamtik I, and the main gallery (which unites the whole into a vast sepulchre) to Ptolemaic times.

Memphis

Little remains of the site of ancient Memphis, the White Wall, Egypt's first capital and one of the most famous and populous capitals of antiquity. What we know of the ancient capital comes largely from the necropolis of Sakkara and from the Step Pyramid complex built by Imhotep for the pharaoh Zoser.

Memphis succumbed to a civil war after the fall of the Old Kingdom, a barbaric invasion by the Hyksos after the fall of the Middle Kingdom, and a shift in centralised power when Thebes became capital in the New Kingdom. It also suffered ransacking by the Libyans, beseiging by the Sudanese, plundering by the Persians, the fanaticism of the early Christians and final destruction at the hands of the Arab conquerors who transported stone slabs, marble and alabaster monuments to lay the foundations of Cairo. The ruins of many temples however, attest to the size of the ancient city. Those of the Temple of Ptah can be traced in its ground-plan some 500 yards to the north of Mit Rahina (a small village near a palm grove). It was here that two colossal statues of Ramses II were found. They probably graced the entrance to the ancient Temple of Ptah in the New Kingdom. One statue, found lying face downwards in the sand and in a perfect state of preservation, was transported to Station Square, Cairo, in 1955; it weighs 65 tons. The other is still in Memphis in a protective structure.

(It should perhaps be mentioned that the ancient city of *On*, the Heliopolitan city of the Sun-god, was also almost totally destroyed. All that remains are the few ruins of the enclosure wall of the Sun Temple and a single obelisk of Aswan granite.)

Dashur

South of Sakkara are the two pyramids of Senefru, the Bent Pyramid and the Northern Pyramid (Chapter 6). On the same plateau there are also two Middle Kingdom pyramids which cannot be compared, in terms of material or construction, with those of the Old Kingdom. They are the pyramids of Senursert III (Sesostris) and Amenemhet II, both brick constructions. The latter is a shapeless black heap of rubble.

Meidum

Some 30 miles south of Dashur are Amenemhet's much ruined Middle Kingdom pyramid (which was built partly of the stone-work—some with relief sculpture—from tombs and monuments of the Old Kingdom), and the remaining core of the first true pyramid (Chapter 6). The statues of Rahotep and Nofert as well as a famous frieze of geese which is a prized possession of the Egyptian Museum were found here.

Beni Hassan

Approaching 'Middle Egypt' one comes, appropriately, to a famous burial ground of the Middle Kingdom. Beni Hassan is famous for the rock-hewn tombs of the 12th-dynasty princes and noblemen. They rank among the most fascinating monuments in Egypt, both for their architectural characteristics (the mastaba form had almost entirely disappeared and these tombs were hewn in a row out of the cliffs, sometimes with rock-cut colonnade at the entrance), and also for the fine representations of domestic life in the Middle Kingdom. Though many of the scenes (such as baking, pottery-making, carpentry, handicrafts, etc) are similar to those depicted at Sakkara, these tombs contain themes not common in the Old Kingdom; for example, youths wrestling, military scenes and an attack on a fortress (tombs of Kheti and Ameni-em-hat). There are also scenes of barbers, washermen, painters, spinning and weaving by women (tomb of Baket), and men felling a palm tree (tomb of Khnumhotep).

Particularly interesting are those scenes which indicate the rising popularity of the cult of Osiris after the fall of the Old Kingdom. In a land of turmoil, Osiris, God of the Underworld, came to represent hope and justice. Thousands of pilgrims travelled from all over the country to attend the annual religious festivals at Abydos, which became the centre of the cult. It became desirable for a wealthy nobleman to construct a second tomb near Abydos, to erect a stele within sight of the august shrine, or be carried, after embalming, to the precincts of the shrine before returning for final interment at his own birthplace. If, for some reason, the pilgrimage could not be performed, then the deceased were meant to make it symbolically, by having the scene represented in their tomb. Such scenes may be seen at Beni Hassan. In the tomb of Khnumhotep a Nile boat bears the mummy of the deceased, accompanied by an inscription that it is being borne to Abydos. The tomb of Amenemhet depicts the deceased, accompanied by his children and harem, travelling in the boat to attend the festival at Abydos, which included the dramatic re-enactment of the life, death and rebirth of Osiris.

Another interesting feature of the tombs of Beni Hassan are the representations of foreigners: a scene of Asiatics, shows men, women and children dressed in gaily coloured national costume and characterised by their hooked noses, sharply cut features and pointed beards. The men in a caravan of Libyans, are distinguished by the ostrich-feathers in their hair, and the women carry baskets on their backs.

The patron deity of Beni Hassan was Bast, the cat-goddess, to whom a temple was started in the 18th dynasty; it was added to in the 19th dynasty but never completed. It is an example of the rock-hewn temple, of which that of Abu Simbel is the largest.

Tel el Amarna

This was the site chosen by Ikhnaton (Amenhotep IV) for his new capital when he rebelled against the priests of Amon in the 18th dynasty, abandoned Thebes and promoted the sole worship of the Aten, the sun-disc. The site was occupied for only about 20 years before the priests of Amon reasserted control and returned the court to Thebes. They regarded Ikhnaton's monotheism as a religious revolution and endeavoured to obliterate all evidence of his reign from the land, razing the temples and palaces in Tel el Amarna; but some of the main streets may still be discerned, as well as the ground-plan of the temple of Aten. The royal family and noblemen fortunately constructed their tombs in the hills to the east of the city. Though in poor condition these contain some of the best surviving examples of the realism characteristic of the 'Amarna period'.

The religious movement of Ikhnaton was accompanied by an artistic revolution which freed the artist from ancient traditions. Paintings and sculpture tended to be more realistic both as regards style and subject matter. The royal family, especially, were represented in a manner totally different from the stylised representations of earlier periods. In one scene, for example, Ikhnaton and Nefertiti, with two young princesses, are seated at a table facing each other. Above them is the symbol of the new religion: the sun with rays extending in hands (tomb of Huye—1). Another depicts the king and the royal family emerging from the palace, inspecting barns and stables attached to the temple, or (accompanied by their daughters) worshipping the sun (tomb of Meri-Re). In the tomb of Iy, favourite of the pharaoh, is a scene of the king and queen at a window of the palace, again accompanied by the young princesses, one of whom touches her mother's chin. They throw decorations to Iy and his wife.

It was at Tel el Amarna that the famous Berlin painted bust of Nefertiti was found, and also the valuable archives on clay tablets, state letters between Amenhotep III and IV and the leaders of Syria, Palestine and Asia.

Abydos

This was one of the most ancient cities in Egypt, which became the centre of the Osiris cult. It was believed that here Isis found the head of Osiris, and buried it (though another version of the myth has her finding the whole body at Abydos with the exception of the phallus which had been eaten by a crocodile).

The earliest tombs at Abydos are pre-dynastic (Chapter 1). There are also the royal tombs of the 1st dynasty (Chapter 2). After the fall of the Old Kingdom and the rise of the cult of Osiris the dead, the city grew and the solemn annual religious festivals included a passion play, enacted by the priests before multitudes in the manner of the Memphite Drama (Chapter 2). It included a ritualistic killing of Osiris by his brother Set, followed by several days of mourning. Funeral wreaths and flowers were placed on the figure of the slain deity as he was borne through the city. The people sang hymns and made offerings and, at a prescribed place in the city, another mock battle took place between the brothers, but this time the murder of Osiris was avenged and a triumphant procession with a risen hero returned to the temple. The whole celebration took eighteen days and the crowning scene was the erection of the backbone of Osiris (the *Dad* fetish) and the placing of his head upon it.

In the New Kingdom, Abydos became a centre of diverse cults. Ptah of Memphis was worshipped there, along with Harmachis and Amon. Seti I started the construction of a temple of the finest-grain limestone, and decorated it in reliefs that are among the finest productions of Egyptian relief sculpture of any age. The temple was completed by Ramses II. Its plan differs from other great Egyptian temples by having not one sanctuary to a single deity, but seven, dedicated to Osiris, Isis, Horus, Ptah, Harmachis, Amon and the deified king himself.

Ramses II also built a temple at Abydos, dedicated to Osiris. Although largely in ruin, this temple appears to have been more carefully constructed than other buildings raised by this pharaoh. Fine-grained limestone was used, with black and red granite for the doorways, sandstone for the columns, and alabaster for an inner shrine. The reliefs are much more crudely executed than those of the temple of Seti I.

Dendera

This is a very ancient religious site and the seat of the worship of Hathor, the cow-goddess. During the New Kingdom, Thutmose II, Ramses II and Ramses III all contributed to the building of the temple of Hathor. The wall reliefs, however, date to a much later period. In fact most of the inscriptions and decorations date from Greco/Roman times and do not compare with the finer work of the earlier periods. Though the temple is constructed in fine symmetry the figures are coarse. Among the Roman Emperors dressed as pharaohs and sacrificing to the gods of Egypt are Augustus, Caligula, Tiberius, Nero and Claudius. On the outer (south) wall is a relief of Caesar, Cleopatra and their son.

The important features of this temple are the eighteen enormous Hathor-headed columns in the Great Hall, a representation of the Sky Goddess Nut with her feet in one corner of the chamber, elongated body across the roof, and feet in the opposite corner, and the chamber in which the Osiris myth is represented in detail. The famous Zodiac in the National Library in Paris was taken from one of the chambers here.

Luxor (Ancient Thebes)

After the war of liberation from the Hyksos, Egypt entered a new phase of development, the New Kingdom. At first the culture differed only slightly from that of the Middle Kingdom, but following the military successes of Thutmose III, who extended Egyptian influence in Western Asia, the political, social and artistic life underwent radical changes. Magnificent treasures poured into Thebes, which became a reservoir of tributes and booty. Since a large share of the wealth was bestowed on the national god, Amon-Ra, enormous temples, elaborately embellished and adorned, were raised in his honour by successive pharaohs. This was a period in which Egypt enjoyed untold power and prestige; when the classical authors Homer, Diodorus, Strabo and Pliny referred to the magnificence of Thebes.

On the eastern bank of the Nile are two great temples, Luxor and Karnak. The Temple of Luxor, built by the 18th-dynasty pharaoh Amenhotep III is one of the most beautiful monuments of the New Kingdom. The clustered papyrus-bud columns of the main court represent a fine example of its architecture. In the main court, surrounded by smooth-shafted papyrus columns with lotus-bud capitals, a Fatimide mosque which was raised to Abu el Hagag still stands. The most important reliefs in this temple are those in the colonnade which depict the great 'Opet' festival when the god Amon was borne in splendid procession from the Temple of Karnak to that of Luxor, and the murals in the Birth Room which show that Amenhotep III ruled by the divine right of the god Amon under the protection of the gods.

Karnak Temple is a huge complex which owes its building to the efforts of successive pharaohs from the Middle Kingdom to the Ptolemaic period (some 2,000 years). Some of its most impressive features are the Great Court, which covers an area of 49,755sq yd and contains a small temple (a perfect example of traditional design) built by Ramses III and a shrine built by Seti II; the Great Hypostyle Hall, its roof supported by 134 columns arranged in sixteen rows, with those of the nave rising to a height of 78ft, and the capitals large enough to hold a hundred men; valuable historical reliefs of the military campaigns of Seti I and Ramses II in Asia (with the actual text of the first non-aggression pact in history, between Ramses II and the Hittite kings); the beautiful obelisk of Queen Haschepsut made of pink Aswan granite, weighing some 700,000lb and, as recorded in the text, quarried and erected in seven months; two granite pillars (in the Hall of Records), one bearing the lotus of Upper Egypt and the other the papyrus of Lower Egypt, and together representing the unity between the 'Two Lands'.

On the western bank of the Nile at Luxor is the necropolis, or city of the dead. Here are a number of mortuary temples including that of Seti I at Kurna (which, like his temple at Abydos, is executed in fine relief), the terraced temple of Queen Haschepsut who is famed, among other things, for her expedition to the Land of Punt to import myrrh and incense trees to be planted in the Great Court, the historically important mortuary temple of Ramses II (the Ramasseum) which contains fragments of his colossus (calculated to have weighed over 2 million pounds) and the complex of Medinet Habu which contains the ruins of temples begun in the 18th dynasty and continuing to Roman times.

The two enormous seated statues known as the Colossi of Memnon are all that remain of the mortuary temple of Amenhotep III. A recent study with nuclear-age technique (neotron activation analysis) has revealed that the quartzite stone for these giant monoliths (each weighing nearly 1·5 million pounds) came from the Gebel El Ahmar quarry near Cairo—nearly 420 miles *downstream*.

The Valley of the Kings is the burial ground of the 18th-, 19th- and 20th-dynasty pharaohs. Their tombs are hewn out of solid rock and inscribed with sacred texts from the Book of the Dead (developed from the Coffin Texts of the Middle Kingdom which were appropriated and revised selections of the Pyramid Texts of the Old Kingdom). The smallest tomb is that of Tutankhamon which was found intact and contained the priceless treasures with which the world is now familiar. The largest belongs to Seti I. It is 100 yards in length and contains fine sculptured wall paintings in perfect preservation. The tomb of Amenhotep II, was found to contain nine royal mummies which had been placed there in sealed chambers for protection. They are now in Cairo Museum along with those recovered from the Shaft at Der el Bahri.

The Valley of the Queens contains the magnificent tomb of Nefer-tari, beloved wife of Ramses II, the tomb of Queen Titi, which has murals in startlingly fresh colour, and the tomb of Ramses III's nine-year-old son who, being under age, is depicted being introduced to the gods of the underworld by his father.

The tombs of the nobles on the Theban necropolis portray the life and times of the New Kingdom. A catalogue of activities may be found in such famous tombs as that of Nakht, Scribe of the Granaries under Thutmose IV, Ramose, Vizier under Amenhotep III and IV, Rekhmire, Vizier under Thutmose III and Amenhotep II, Sennofer, Overseer of the Gardens of Amon under Amenhotep II, Mena, Scribe of the Fields under Thutmose IV and many more. There are well over 300 tombs of New Kingdom noblemen, almost all of which were painted on specially prepared limestone surfaces. In contrast to the massive, stylised portrayals of pharaohs and deities on the sculpted walls of the national temples, these paintings are naturalistic.

Der el Medina is a small, graceful Ptolemaic temple on the Theban necropolis.

Esna

Esna, an important monastic centre in the early Christian era, contains the ruins of the Temple to Khnum, the ram-headed god who was believed to have fashioned man on a potter's wheel from the clay of the Nile. The temple dates to the Ptolemaic period (though it was built on the site of an earlier temple raised by the 18th-dynasty pharaoh Thutmose III). Some sections of the temple were constructed and adorned by the Romans. The main columned hall contains representations of the Roman Emperors dressed as pharaohs, worshipping Egyptian deities. The cartouches bear the names Marcus Aurelius, Antoninus Pius, Claudius and Decius.

Edfu

One of the most perfectly preserved monuments in Egypt is to be found here. It is the Temple of Horus, constructed of sandstone. The main temple was begun by Ptolemy III in 237 BC on the site of an earlier shrine. It was enlarged during successive reigns until 57 BC, when it was given a final touch. The history of its construction along with a detailed description of the temple is inscribed on the outer face of the girdle wall. The predominant theme of the reliefs is the pharaoh (Ptolemy Soter II or Ptolemy Alexander) consorting with the Egyptian deities and triumphing over the enemies. Apart from the faces, which were damaged by the early Christians, the murals are perfectly preserved.

Kom Ombo

Ombos was a pre-dynastic settlement. It was only in the Ptolemaic era that it attained prosperity and temples were constructed (on the sites of earlier shrines of which little is now left). The Temple of Sobek and Haroeris was built on a uniform plan typical of the Ptolemaic period and, like the temples of Dendera, Edfu and Philae, was decorated with reliefs of several Ptolemaic kings and Roman emperors. The murals in low relief dating from the Greek era can easily be distinguished from the Roman, which are in high. The most beautiful reliefs are in the Great Hypostyle Hall where the king (Neos Dionysos) is depicted before Haroeris, whilst being blessed by the lion-headed Selket and the hawk-headed Harsiesis.

Aswan

Aswan was the departure point for the great caravan routes to the south and the area where the powerful noblemen of the Old Kingdom kept the border with Nubia. Unlike Luxor which grew into an important metropolis, Aswan retained its trading-post aura. Situated partly on the plain and partly on a hill, it commands a view of exceptional beauty where the Nile divides into several arms separated by islands of granite. In the 1950s this was where the Aga Khan wintered, along with the rest of Europe's notables who found it the world's most desirable escape from winter.

The granite quarries at Aswan, the source of the finest quality granite for tomb and temple building, were exploited from the early dynasties through to Roman times. A huge unfinished obelisk in the northern quarry, on which the under-cutting was never completed, would, if raised, have been taller than Haschepsut's obelisk at Karnak; 95 feet against 92.

The rock tombs at Aswan date for the most part from the close of the Old Kingdom and from the Middle Kingdom. The tomb of Harkhuf, the first explorer (Chapter 4), who brought back a dwarf for his pharaoh (Chapter 7), is situated here. One of the best-preserved tombs is that of prince Siren-powet (Middle Kingdom) which contains interesting family scenes.

In antiquity the whole area surrounding and including the island of Elephantine was known as Yebu, or Elephant Land. On the southern section of the island are the ruins of the ancient town. There is also an ancient nilometer (Chapter 2) and the foundations of a temple constructed of stones brought from earlier temples. The Kalabsha Temple, the largest detached structure in Nubia, dating from the time of the late Ptolemies and the Emperor Augustus, has been dismantled and reconstructed on a new site in Aswan to save it from flooding by the Nile due to the Aswan Dam scheme. Official inauguration of the reconstructed temple took place in 1975.

Philae

The island of Philae, which holds some seventeen temples dating between the 26th dynasty and the Greco-Roman period, lay under water for six months each year following the construction of the Aswan Dam. Action to save the monuments was first taken in 1965 by the Ministry of Culture in collaboration with UNESCO. During the first stage over 1,000 iron sheet curtains were driven into the Nile to mark the boundaries of a temporary dam encircling the island. Then 366,000 cubic yards of sand was filled into the course of the dam, the intention being to keep the Nile waters from the land in order that the monuments could be cleaned prior to their eventual removal. Work is now taking place on the final stage of levelling and resurfacing the new site for the Philae Temples on Agilca island, and dismantling fourteen of the temples started in May 1975.

The main temples are dedicated to the goddess Isis and her son Horus (the walls are filled with reliefs depicting Ptolemaic and Roman emperors at sacrificial ceremonies). Other monuments on Philae include a temple to Hathor, the Kiosk which is one of the finest buildings on the island, the Arch of Hadrian, the Temple of Harendotes and the ruins of a Temple of Augustus, among others.

Abu Simbel

This great rock temple, built by Ramses II, is the largest in Nubia and one of the most impressive and famous memorials of ancient Egypt. It is carved out of living rock and at the entrance four seated colossi of Ramses II, each 66 feet high, together with smaller statues of members of the royal family, form the entrance. Ramses II is one of the central figures in Egyptian history. Although responsible for but one great battle and one great peace alliance, he raised so many inspiring monuments to the glory of his ancestors (some of which were indisputably better rulers and conquerors) and had himself portrayed in such huge statues, that he has gone down in history as one of the greatest of Egyptian pharaohs.

The temple of Abu Simbel (at its new site above the waters of Lake Nasser) is so oriented that the rising sun casts its first rays through the entrance, down a double row of statues of Ramses in Osirian form clasping crook and flail, and through to the sanctuary where he sits in the company of the gods Ra, Ptah and Amon.

In following the Nile upstream we have briefly outlined the chief monuments in the Nile valley; the material relics of the ancient civilisation. In the rural areas of Egypt, however, we see the peasant farmers with sturdy-bodies and almond-shaped eyes strangely reminiscent of the murals of the tombs of Sakkara that we have described. They still plough the fields with oxen, harvest the crop with sickle and use a winnowing fork to sift the grain. Their villages are largely of sun-dried brick. The buffalo and donkey are still their faithful companions. Geese swim in the ponds and canals where migratory birds settle for a short time before taking once again to the air. Fishermen cast their drag-nets, trawl-nets or wicker baskets. The dykes between fields serve as paths. And the plant forms that influenced ancient Egyptian architecture, the papyrus, lotus and reed, can still be seen growing in abundance. Largely barren Upper Egypt still has economic ties with the south, while the fertile, cosmopolitan Delta looks to the countries of the Mediterranean.

Books Recommended for Further Reading

Aldred, C. *Old Kingdom Art in Ancient Egypt* (London, 1949)

Edwards, I. E. S. *The Pyramids of Egypt* (rev ed, London, 1960)

Emery, W. B. *Archaic Egypt* (Harmondsworth, 1961, rep 1972)

Faulkner, R. O. *The Pyramid Texts* (Cambridge University Press, 1971)

Gardiner, Sir Alan. *Egypt of the Pharaohs* (Oxford University Press, rep 1972)

Hayes, W. C. *The Sceptre of Egypt*, 2 vols (New York & Cambridge, Mass, 1953–9)

Kamil, Jill. *Luxor—A Guide to Ancient Thebes* (London, 2nd ed, 1976)

Lichtheim, M. *Ancient Egyptian Literature* (University of California Press, 1973)

Mendelssohn, Kurt. *The Riddle of the Pyramids* (London, 1974).

Wilson, John A. *The Culture of Ancient Egypt* (University of Chicago Press, 1956)

Acknowledgement

To the late Dr Abdel Moneim Abu Bakr, Professor of Egyptian Archaeology, Cairo University, who read the manuscript and made valuable suggestions.

Index